Maids of Honor

by Joan Casademont

SAMUEL FRENCH, INC.
45 West 25th Street   NEW YORK 10010
7623 Sunset Boulevard   HOLLYWOOD 90046
LONDON   *TORONTO*

IMPORTANT BILLING AND CREDIT REQUIREMENTS

All producers of MAIDS OF HONOR *must* give credit to the Author of the Play in all programs distributed in connection with performances of the Play and in all instances in which the title of the Play appears for purposes of advertising, publicizing or otherwise exploiting the Play and/or a production. The name of the Author *must* also appear on a separate line, on which no other name appears, immediately following the title, and *must* appear in size of type not less than fifty percent the size of the title type.

The following credit must also appear in all programs distributed in connection with performances of the play and in all instances in which the play is advertised, publicized or otherwise exploited:

"Originally produced by the WPA Theatre in New York City, 1990, Kyle Renick, Artistic Director."

Maids of Honor premiered at the WPA Theatre in New York City in June, 1990 where it was directed by Max Mayer. The cast (in order of appearance):

ISABELLE BOWLIN.........Elizabeth McGovern
ANNIE BOWLIN...................Kyra Sedgwick
MONICA BOWLIN.....................Laila Robins
PAT WEINHARDT................Kristine Nielsen
HARRY HOBSON..........John Michael Higgins
JOEL SILVERMAN.....................Jake Weber
ROGER DOWLING........................Joe Urla

Setting by Edward T. Gianfrancesco
Lighting by Craig Evans
Costume Design by Mimi Maxmen
Sound by Aural Fixation
Casting by Chavanne/Mossberg
Production Stage Manager Denise Laffer

CHARACTERS

ISABELLE (IZZY) BOWLIN, 27, the youngest
   sister
ANNIE BOWLIN, 30, the middle sister
MONICA BOWLIN, 33, the eldest sister
PAT WEINHARDT, 33, Monica's best friend
HARRY HOBSON, 32, Annie's old fiance
JOEL SILVERMAN, 25, a reporter, Izzy's friend
ROGER DOWLING, 34, Monica's ex-boyfriend

SETTING

The spacious kitchen and side porch of the
Bowlin sisters' childhood house, the day before
and the day of Monica's wedding, which is to
have an outside garden reception. The kitchen is
orderly and sparsely furnished with New England
wood furniture. A long big table and chairs
occupies the center, and there is an exit to the side
porch that has a screen door. The porch faces an
unseen reception tent, and there is a stretch of
seen lawn inbetween porch and tent. In the
kitchen, there is another exit to steps that lead
upstairs. These steps are in a partially-seen foyer.

TIME

The present, in the spring, in a small
Massachusetts town on the North Shore.

ACT I

Scene 1

The kitchen is empty for a brief moment. Late afternoon light streams in the windows. A tall, thin and wired young woman, IZZY, enters in a hurry from within the house, by the back steps. She wears sneakers and a very fancy white wedding dress which appears thrown on over her clothes. There is a coffee stain on the front of the dress that SHE tries to wipe off with Kleenex. SHE hurriedly checks out the porch to make sure the coast is clear, shuts the door to the porch, closes the shutters on the door and back windows and dashes to the refrigerator. Frantically SHE searches for bubbly water but can't find it. We see ANNIE, a much softer-looking woman, enter from the porch and look behind her thoughtfully at the yard. SHE has been out walking and drinks from a big bottle of mineral water as SHE collects herself to enter the house with a purpose. SHE catches IZZY off guard as SHE enters through the porch door.

IZZY. Ah! Watch it, will ya!

ANNIE. (*Gaping.*) Izzy, you're wearing her wedding dress.

IZZY. Correct. (*Tries to hide the stain, moves away, mortified.*)

7

ANNIE. (*Circling.*) Do you comprehend that under the circumstances, putting on the dress before the ceremony must and will insure more bad luck?!

IZZY. (*Trying to joke.*) Only for the bride.

ANNIE. Take it off! Get it the hell off that body immediately!

IZZY. Okay! God! (*Turning so that ANNIE can unbutton, still covering the stain.*) Try to stay calm, Annie. Try to stay calm.

ANNIE. I am perfectly calm. I mean, I would be calm if you would control your impulses! She could walk in any minute!

IZZY. White isn't my color anyway, I've seen enough. (*IZZY steps out of the dress, hangs it over a chair carefully, still trying to cover the stain. She wears a T-shirt and shorts.*) Did you make a decision on your walk?

ANNIE. No.

IZZY. Why not?!

ANNIE. Because it is a very hard decision! It is a very, very, very hard decision! Do you understand?

IZZY. You're saying it's a very hard decision.

ANNIE. Right.

IZZY. Could I uh—borrow your water?

ANNIE. What for?

IZZY. (*Shrugs.*) Eh!

ANNIE. Did you—you didn't stain that wedding dress, did you?!

IZZY. A teeny little spot, some fizzy water and it'll be history!

ANNIE. Oh, my God! Oh, my God, how could this happen?! (*SHE plops the water onto the table, collapses into a chair with her head in her hands.*)

IZZY. (*Grabs the water, getting napkins.*) It was an accident!

ANNIE. It's a nightmare!

IZZY. (*Struggling to get the spot out.*) It'll come out, look, it's coming out, it's going, it's gone, it's gone!

ANNIE. We can't tell her.

IZZY. It's out, why mention it?

ANNIE. She simply cannot be told that her fiance is going to be arrested the day before her wedding. My brain is screaming, I can't handle it, and if I can't handle it, neither could she.

IZZY. Maybe you need a few more minutes to consider that we really don't have an alternative.

ANNIE. Christ, we really don't, do we?! (*ANNIE circles the room, taking deep breaths and trying to calm herself. Pause.*)

IZZY. Famous talk show host weds Wall Street hotshot of the century. If Mom were still alive, her eyes would cross from finally being able to look down her nose at so many people.

ANNIE. Lemme at least get it straight. Chuck has been accepting bribes of millions for insider trading tips. *The Globe* is running the story in two days, and then Chuck will be arrested.

IZZY. Bingo. Put behind bars like a hairy animal.

ANNIE. Somebody in this family has to go on and make a successful marriage!

IZZY. This is your idea of a successful marriage?! (*Pause.*) Tell me the truth, Annie. Do you think she loves him?

ANNIE. (*Rising.*) Let's just stick to the problem at hand. (*Pause.*) I can't tell her!

IZZY. She has got to know she's marrying a scumbag criminal!

ANNIE. Then you do it!

IZZY. She'd kill me! Not to mention that she'd never believe me, but she'd kill me anyway!

ANNIE. There'd be a murder in this house after all! That is not a good idea!

IZZY. (*Pause.*) Did Monica tell you that she hired Harry's catering service?

ANNIE. What does that have to do with anything?!

IZZY. I think Harry still loves you. Even Monica knows that!

ANNIE. I don't want to talk about Harry, and I certainly don't think he will show up here, do you?

IZZY. Probably!

ANNIE. Oh, he will not! Besides, that has nothing to do with anything!

(*IZZY sits close to ANNIE, who won't look at her. Pause.*)

IZZY. Boy, it's good to see you. I've missed you so much! You live so far away, I almost drove my car off a bridge when I thought you weren't coming!

ANNIE. Why wouldn't I come? It's Monica's wedding. I hope.

IZZY. This family. Surprise, ambush, attack. Was there ever any reason?

ANNIE. That's behind us, Izzy. We're adults and that's supposed to be behind us now!

IZZY. Are you gonna tell her what she has to know?

ANNIE. I can't tell her, that's my final decision!

IZZY. Think of it this way. There she is, married to mister Wall Street catch of the century, livin' in her triplex, havin' her face inflicted upon thousands of homes around the country via the TV, maybe with one or two perfect children and one or two perfect vacation homes and one day five cop cars come screaming up to the station. Ten guys in helmets, shiny badges and guns in holsters storm into the studio. Monica's in front of the cameras, taping with an audience of hundreds, just about to ask Doctor Ruth if she'd recommend that masturbation replace the sex act completely anyway because after all it would be simpler, and bang, the handcuffs are on her. They haul her off, kicking and yelping, destroying her hairdo completely. Shortly thereafter Chuck's thrown into the slammer for ten years and Monica's found guilty of conspiracy for withholding information. This could be very upsetting to her.

ANNIE. Izzy, you're gonna give me a heart attack!

IZZY. Her career is over!

ANNIE. Don't even say that!

IZZY. Marrying a scumbag sleazeball toad of a criminal is gonna fuckin' demolish the credibility of a talk show host who brags about being a serious reporter!

ANNIE. Shit!

IZZY. Exactly.

ANNIE. (*Jumping up.*) Oh, all right, all right, I'll tell her! But when, Izzy, when? Tonight's the rehearsal dinner, all these people are already in town, the wedding's tomorrow, do you understand? Tomorrow!

IZZY. Guess you better tell her now!

ANNIE. Now?!

IZZY. As soon as she comes in.

ANNIE. As soon as she comes in?
IZZY. You'll do it?
ANNIE. I'll try!

(There is the sound of LAUGHTER around the side of the house and MONICA, a very attractive and jumpy woman appears on the porch carrying shopping bags with PAT, a New York socialite. Both IZZY and ANNIE jump. A loud whisper:)

ANNIE. Get that dress outta here!

(ANNIE slams her glass down, shoves the dress at IZZY, who tears out of the room with it and up the steps as PAT opens the door for MONICA and they enter.)

PAT. Well, walkin' around downtown with this sister of yours is like walkin' around with Princess Di, I swear!
MONICA. Oh, how I do enjoy the fantasy when I see that the Cecily Hills of this world have gone no farther than next door and have accomplished no more than reproduction. Those people know shit about what really goes down in this world! And I used to feel intimidated? Christ!
PAT. Cecily Hill got so intimidated at the sight of the TV princess here she led her own children into traffic!
ANNIE. No!
PAT. Caused a three-car pile up. A few injuries, no deaths. Glimpse a princess, forsake your children.
MONICA. Please! What's this princess stuff, Pat? We didn't exactly come from royalty, did we, Annie? *(MONICA goes to Annie, gives her a hug and a kiss.)*

ANNIE. You can say that again!

MONICA. Well, here we are, this is it, I'm finally gettin' hitched! Dear. Unfortunate phrasing. You excited?!

ANNIE. (*Trying hard.*) Sure! It's exciting! (*ANNIE leans on the counter, drinks her water.*)

MONICA. (*MONICA arranges her bags awkwardly. Pause.*) Is everything all right?

ANNIE. (*Strained.*) Fine.

PAT. Well I know that not only didn't you come from royalty, you came from the trash heap socially. I mean just socially, of course! Me too! That's why I married the right to spit in every one of their eyes! Anyway, Annie, you should see 'em out there. We go up one street and people part like waves, buzzin' about her TV show, wanting autographs for their paraplegic nephew or some damn heartbreaking thing, we go down another street and it's my enemies from that two-bit yacht club oohin' and aahin' 'cause she's about to marry one of Wall Street's most important and handsome investment bankers, we go into a shop and the salesgirl is some townie person we went to junior high school with who's still enthralled by your sister's aura, just like everybody was back then. You don't need blue blood to get yourself an aura. It's all about your bank account anyway. You want a drink, Monica?

MONICA. I'm fine, thanks.

PAT. I sure need one after all that hoopla and more to come. Not that it isn't fun. I adore social revenge. Annie?

ANNIE. I'm fine too, Pat.

PAT. It's gin and tonic for me, I experienced so much pleasure out there I may start to experience some guilt!

MONICA. (*Meaning the booze.*) That'll fend it off.

PAT. Keeps me nasty!

*(ANNIE and MONICA laugh. PAT goes to liquor cabinet
and fridge as if they were hers, pulls out gin, tonic, ice,
a glass.)*

MONICA. Lately I'm abstaining from just about
everything anyway, have you noticed, Annie?

PAT. God, I sure have! No booze, no pills, no
cigarettes, no sugar, no red meat, no caffeine. Christ, girl,
no fun!

ANNIE. Why so disciplined?

MONICA. Statistics! Ordinary people do not know how
many unexpected food substances, chemicals and by-
products are being discovered dangerous on a daily basis. I
interview all the experts! Did you see my show two weeks
ago on alcoholism and heredity?

ANNIE. You know I don't get it at home, but I'd love
to—

MONICA. I'll give you the tape. It was such a good
show, one of my best! Get this! The latest poop from the
top is that there may in fact be an alcoholic gene that
certain children of alcoholics inherit, which explains why
there are so many alcoholics among—oh, you don't really
wanna know about this today, do you?

PAT. Definitely not.

MONICA. If I could just learn how to escape my own
brain I'd be fine. Is Izzy here yet?

ANNIE. Upstairs. She'll be right down. The tent looks
wonderful, Monica. Everything looks so beautiful!

MONICA. *(MONICA pulls her shoes off, rubs her
feet.)* You really think so?

ANNIE. Yes!

PAT. It ought to, this is a top of the line shindig for a top of the line gal.

MONICA. I see those bills and all I can think is, thank God he's richer than I am!

PAT. The only reason to marry.

MONICA. (*Embarrassed.*) An okay reason. What about those orchids, Annie?

ANNIE. What about them?

MONICA. Don't they seem kinda—pretentious or something? I don't know, I got kinda sick looking at them just now.

ANNIE. There are several.

PAT. Two thousand fifty-eight, to be exact.

ANNIE. No!

MONICA. I'm not convinced it doesn't look like I'm just knockin' my brains out to prove something. I mean that is the name of the game today but I don't wanna reek of it.

PAT. Go ahead and reek!

MONICA. They were Mom's favorite, but I don't even know if people like orchids, do they Annie?

PAT. Have a drink, Monica. Why vacuum all the fun outta your life?

MONICA. Maybe just a tiny one. Mostly tonic.

(*PAT makes Monica a drink. ANNIE sits.*)

ANNIE. The orchids definitely transform the yard from a nondescript square of grass into a beautiful and exotic place.

MONICA. Yeah ...

ANNIE. That's what you said you wanted.

MONICA. I never know what I really, really want.

PAT. Oh, now, come on, Monica, you do too! We all know your poor deceased mother—who I loved like my own, I did—always wanted one of her girls to have a garden wedding right here in her home. You haven't sold the house yet, it makes perfect sense.

MONICA. It's creepy to be in this old house. This creepy old house that's rented out to strangers.

ANNIE. Well, look, if we hadn't hung onto it we wouldn't all be here for the reception of Mom's dreams!

IZZY. (*Comes down the back steps, enters talking.*) Only it ain't Ma's wedding, is it?

MONICA. (*Jumping up, delighted.*) Izzy! (*MONICA runs to her, kisses and hugs her.*) Oh, I'm so glad you're here!

IZZY. I was forced to come, I'm one of the maids of honor.

MONICA. (*Slapping her on the arm, playful.*) Thanks.

IZZY. Hi, Pat. I'll have one of those.

PAT. Hello, Isabelle.

(*THEY kiss cheeks.*)

PAT. Now here's a woman after my own heart. Izzy, tell your sister she's made all the right decisions.

IZZY. (*Caught off guard.*) Uh—how do you mean?

PAT. How do I mean?! I mean everything. Won't two-thousand fifty-eight orchids make people black and blue with envy? (*PAT gives Monica her drink, makes Izzy's.*)

IZZY. That why she picked orchids?

PAT. Well no, but it's a fringe benefit.

MONICA. I just wanted to make that old yard look beautiful. I thought about roses, I made specific trips here to just stand outside in the yard by myself and visualize roses. Those new neighbors to the back must've thought I was nuts, they'd be peekin' out their windows at me and I'd be standing in the middle of the yard with my fists clenched and my eyes shut for twenty-minute periods. This weird and very spooky thing would happen to me every time I'd shut my eyes hard and say, "roses." All of a sudden I'd get these flashes—like real-life visions of Mom as a little girl with pink orchids in her hair standing right in front of me in the yard. I just said, to hell with it, give in to the orchids, jerk!, realizing how happy they'd make her. I mean, I do think they're just what Mom would've wanted ... (*MONICA breaks off and bursts into tears with a whine.*) Ohh, nooo ... (*SHE pulls out a handkerchief, hides her face.*)

ANNIE. (*Jumping up, trying to comfort her.*) Oh, dear. Monica? Now Monica ...

IZZY. Shit.

PAT. What's she cryin' about? Honey, you have nothing to cry about, let me cry.

ANNIE. It's normal to have doubts, Monica, it's okay.

PAT. What?! She couldn't find a better catch!

IZZY. I hate that word "catch"! It belongs only in reference to fish!

PAT. Then Chuck is a goddamn whale if you know what I'm saying.

MONICA. Pat, please.

ANNIE. Maybe you should lie down before dinner, Monica. Do you wanna—

IZZY. Lie down?! Annie, we don't have time to—

ANNIE. Would you let me handle it, Izzy?!

PAT. Don't have her lying down. She should talk it out. Now what is it, Monica honey, what's wrong?

MONICA. Happiness ... stress ... my feet ... Guilt about liking roses better than orchids ... Mom's life was so sad ... (*SHE cries again.*)

ANNIE. (*Comforts her.*) Now, now, Monica, Mom died happy! Remember how happy she was when she left for that trip?

MONICA. (*Sniffling.*) Yes ...

PAT. Can you imagine being hit on the head by falling rocks when you were just tryin' to climb some damn mountain in Tibet?! What a tragedy! That poor lovely woman flew halfway around the world for spiritual reasons I cannot fathom only to be bumped off by foreign rocks?! I could just shoot God for that one!

IZZY. Pat. You make me look sensitive.

PAT. What do you mean, this is empathy! (*SHE takes a swig of her drink.*)

MONICA. (*Amused in spite of herself.*) I'm okay! You can argue! (*SHE composes herself. To Annie:*) Thanks.

IZZY. Sorry to tell you this Monica, but Annie has something pressing to tell you that's REALLY gonna make you cry.

ANNIE. Izzy!

MONICA. (*Panicky.*) What's she saying?

ANNIE. (*To Izzy.*) Oo, you make me mad!

IZZY. What are you waiting for, a personal visitation from Christ?

MONICA. Annie, what?

(*Pause.*)

ANNIE. Pat, would you mind if Izzy and I had a few minutes alone with Monica?

PAT. Not so long as whatever you have to say doesn't change anything that's about to happen. Of course it won't, right?

IZZY. Of course not.

PAT. Jealousy is perfectly understandable to me under these and any circumstances but look at it like inheriting a family bank that charges no interest. (*SHE winks at Monica.*) I'll be out back.

ANNIE. Thanks, Pat.

(*PAT exits with the bottle.*)

MONICA. What on earth do you have to tell me? If it's about Roger I don't wanna hear it.

IZZY. It's not!

MONICA. Is it about the wedding? Annie? What is all this?!

IZZY. Calm down, Monica. Everything's gonna be okay.

MONICA. Wanna make me hysterical? Tell me to calm down. Annie?

ANNIE. Uhh—well ... Uhh—well you know first of all that we are not jealous to an unhealthy degree or anything, Monica.

MONICA. Of course not. Pat's the one who wants to throw herself off a tall building since I got engaged. She means it as a compliment!

IZZY. All I ever hear about is Chuck's bank account. Does he have a personality?

MONICA. You don't like him?

IZZY. I can't find him, he's buried under his income.

ANNIE. Izzy, would you let me handle it.

IZZY. Just handle it already!

MONICA. Boy, I don't like this!

(*Pause.*)

ANNIE. So anyway Monica you know we want each other to be happy because we've just been through too much shit not to, and we are all very sensitive, probably overly sensitive, to how important it is to make a good marriage.

MONICA. Oh, yes. Christ, yes! (*As SHE goes to the liquor, pours herself a hefty drink:*) There are times when a person shouldn't be so goddamn long-winded, Annie.

IZZY. Since when are you packing it in?

ANNIE. Izzy!

MONICA. (*To Izzy.*) I do not pack it in! (*SHE takes a swig.*) For your information, I haven't had one drink in three months. Besides, I have certainly researched the subject of booze more than anyone in this room, and have good reason to believe that if you are clean for three hundred sixty-three days of the year, it is pretty damn safe to run a little amok for the other two. Even if you go berserk, which I certainly do not plan on doing.

IZZY. Who ever PLANS on going berserk?

ANNIE. AS I was saying!

MONICA. The point, Annie, please! (*MONICA drinks.*)

ANNIE. We—well we all thought you'd marry Roger, I mean, you were in love with Roger, you lived with him, you knew him well and everything. One day you move out and only three months later it's this guy Chuck. What happened?

MONICA. I said I didn't wanna talk about Roger and I meant it. Would you guys forget Roger even exists, please?

ANNIE. Fine.

MONICA. Two years I lived with the man, we fought about everything, we went to couples therapy, we tried. He doesn't wanna have children until I'm a hundred, I want kids soon and so does Chuck, we work together. Now what is it you have to tell me.

ANNIE. It's not about Roger anyway.

IZZY. So Chuck's gonna make such a great Daddy-o? His ex-wife told a friend of mine at the paper that he can't even have children, there's something wrong with his dick, that's why he's over forty and has none!

MONICA. That is a vicious lie!

IZZY. My friend didn't think so!

MONICA. Izzy! Izzy, that is the most ridiculous thing I've ever heard! I know for a fact that there is nothing wrong with Chuck's equipment! Don't you think I've found out? For god's sakes, if you wanna make it as a reporter you're gonna have to learn to never listen to the ex-wives! Christ!

ANNIE. Monica, what we have to tell you is not about Roger, and it has nothing to do with anyone's equipment.

MONICA. I am not in the mood for games. Who?!

IZZY. Chuck!

MONICA. Oh, boy. Cheers! (*SHE tries to down the drink, stops with a little choke.*) Yecch! That's disgusting to me now, isn't that great? (*SHE puts it down.*) So what is it? He doesn't drink, he shows no violent tendencies, the only thing that works him into a lather is money! (*Pause.*) Well, I'm not repeating in any way, am I?

ANNIE. No!

IZZY. How do you know?

ANNIE. Not in those ways!

IZZY. (*Blurts.*) He's a crook!

ANNIE. Izzy!

MONICA. What?!

ANNIE. Izzy, how could you—

IZZY. You take too long!

MONICA. Our father wasn't a crook too, was he?!

IZZY. Who knows!

ANNIE. Izzy, you have no control!

IZZY. I could age ten years waiting for you to finish a sentence!

MONICA. Wait a minute. Just wait a minute. Are you telling me that Chuck, Charles Stockwell, my fiance, the man I'm going to marry tomorrow, is a crook?!

ANNIE. Unfortunately it looks that way, yes.

MONICA. Embezzling, tax evasion, robbery, what?

IZZY. Insider trading, huge pay-offs for tips on mergers.

MONICA. Where'd you get this information?

IZZY. Joel Silverman, the new star investigative reporter who I work for at the paper.

MONICA. Is the Globe definitely running it?

IZZY. I think so. I mean yes. Monday. I mean— Sunday.

(*Pause.*)

MONICA. (*With a laugh.*) She does not know what she's talking about. Annie?! Do you hear this? Some half-baked nitwit at her paper heard some rumor about my very high profile, very rich fiance who he's probably insanely jealous of, so he's making it into a story so he can impress a secretary at his paper?!

IZZY. Secretary?! Annie, do you hear this?! She's accusing me of being a secretary!

ANNIE. You are a secretary!

IZZY. Every chance she gets she tries to belittle me by reminding me that I'm a secretary!

MONICA. This is total bullshit! This man has no sources on Chuck, does he?

ANNIE. Please talk to her directly.

IZZY. Keep slingin' the shit Monica, but I asked Joel to stop by this house late tonight, after the rehearsal dinner, because I knew you would just put me down and walk all over my face for tryin' to warn you about who you're marrying 'cause it's gonna mess up your life! Christ!

(*Pause.*)

MONICA. Well now let's look at this thing. If there is any truth in it whatsoever, it's not murder or anything, I mean it's an understandable crime. In my business you certainly get to know the difference. We did a show on the families of unsolved murders, you know, people who were just nailed for nothing, the police can't find any motives? God, that's tragic. Made me feel lucky.

IZZY. Joel has sources. I might be a piece of shit to you, but he knows what he's doing.

MONICA. Izzy, you are not a piece of shit, you shouldn't even say things like that.

IZZY. That's right, you'll say them for me.

MONICA. Annie?! Did I call her a piece of shit or did I merely imply that she was—unprofessional? Look in the dictionary! Under "unprofessional" they do not have the words, "piece of shit."

ANNIE. Monica?!

(Pause.)

MONICA. Well, anyway, it's just not THAT bad. Murder, child molestation, sexual perversion, would be very, very bad. This is manageable. This doesn't even necessarily mean I can't marry him. I'm not even gonna think about it until I have the proof right here in front of me. Doesn't that make sense?

ANNIE. Fine!

(IZZY shoots Annie a look.)

MONICA. Chuck is still a very good man, he's very interested in fatherhood.

IZZY. A man who would lie to his business partners would lie to his marriage partner.

MONICA. Oh, you are so naive! Neither marriage nor business is about always telling the absolute truth, and your chances of finding a soul mate in either arena are slim to nill.

IZZY. Why not marry someone who you find physically repulsive? That way you'd never even be tempted to mix business with pleasure!

MONICA. I'm thirty-three years old going on fifty-three. I want a family that functions efficiently, like other people have! I'm sick of having to fight so hard all the time!

ANNIE. Monica this isn't your last chance.

(Pause.)

MONICA. Fine. Okay, fine. Look, let's just forget this now and get ready for tonight. (*MONICA gets her packages.*)

(An attractive, lumbering MAN appears on the porch, dressed in a nice sports jacket. ANNIE knows who it is immediately at the sound of his voice.)

MONICA. Now Annie, you know I've hired—
HARRY. (*Calls.*) Hello!
ANNIE. (*Panicked.*) Harry! Oh my God!

(SHE tries to make a bee-line for the back steps but IZZY blocks her.)

IZZY. (*A loud whisper.*) Annie, what is wrong with you?!
ANNIE. Outta my way!
IZZY. No!
HARRY. Anyone home?

(HE appears at the screen door before ANNIE can exit. THEY freeze. MONICA puts down her packages, checks her appearance.)

MONICA. Harry!
HARRY. (*Through the door.*) Hiya, Monica. Is Annie around?

(*MONICA opens the door.*)

HARRY. (*Enters, spots her.*) Annie! There she is!

(*HE goes to her with open arms, SHE moves backwards, HE stops.*)

HARRY. Good to see you.
ANNIE. Yeah. Same.
IZZY. (*With open arms, as old pals.*) Harold!
HARRY. Isabelle!

(*THEY hug each other.*)

HARRY. How've you been? You look wonderful!
IZZY. Good! And you! Look at you! You gotta be middle-aged by now and you're still a stud!
HARRY. Oh, right! Just how I think of myself, in both categories!
IZZY. Look at him, Annie! Isn't he still studly?
ANNIE. (*Trying to smile.*) Izzy ...
HARRY. She never thought so anyway, that's why I asked her to the prom.
ANNIE. You never asked me to a prom.
HARRY. I meant to! (*To Monica:*) Have you gotten a chance to try those couple of extra dishes I sent over?

MONICA. Uh—well, no, not yet, Harry, but I didn't know you yourself would personally be doing the catering.

HARRY. I always oversee the big events. What bigger event could there be than a Bowlin marriage?

MONICA. (*With a laugh.*) It is more important than international news, that's for sure.

HARRY. It is in my book. (*MONICA gives him a look.*) So I have a small book, sue me. No, don't sue me. Just give the food to the dogs and I won't charge you if you don't like it.

ANNIE. Look, uh—we have to get changed for the rehearsal dinner, so I'm heading up!

HARRY. If now's a bad time, I could check things—

(*ANNIE exits up the back steps, fast. Pause.*)

HARRY. Later ... in another lifetime ...

IZZY. (*A loud whisper to Harry.*) Deep down she's thrilled to see you! I know!

HARRY. Just the feeling I got.

IZZY. Lemme talk to her! Just hold on, lemme talk some sense into her! (*IZZY exits up steps.*)

(*MONICA and HARRY look at each other helplessly.*)

MONICA. Talk to me about food.

BLACKOUT

End Scene 1

Scene 2

Late that night, after the rehearsal dinner and toasts.
ANNIE, IZZY and MONICA are very dressed up.
MONICA in particular looks weary and tipsy from the
evening and sits drinking straight from a bottle of good
vodka at one end of the table. IZZY sits smoking
cigarettes at the far end of the table and drinking.
ANNIE leans on the counter, nervously eating peaches
from a basket. JOEL SILVERMAN, an earnest and
quick young man dressed in ragged prep, sits across
from Monica. There is a briefcase by his feet.

MONICA. Lemme get this straight. You, a grown
man—or at least a semi-grown man—have come here
tonight expecting to be embraced as a kind of angel of
mercy for telling me some hokey story about my fiance
and then admitting that you're not entirely sure that the
paper is running it yet?! Are you some kind of masochist?

JOEL. Look, I—must have been unclear. They will run
the story. They will definitely run the story because it's
true.

MONICA. That's not what you just said.

JOEL. What did I just say?

MONICA. You just said that you hoped they would run
it on Sunday. Wonder what the hold up is about.

JOEL. It's about one final confirmation call that I'll
receive tonight or tomorrow morning at the latest, but the
story is written, it's been reviewed by the lawyers, my
editor is just waiting for my call which I will make at the

very latest tomorrow morning after I get the confirmation call.

MONICA. How old are you?

JOEL. I—don't know what that has to do with this story.

IZZY. Monica, he's put his ass on the line to do you a fuckin' favor, do you have to chew on him?

JOEL. Isabelle, I can handle it.

MONICA. Can you now? You know what I think? I've been in the news business a fuck of a lot longer than you have and I don't think you're prepared for just how far your ass is gonna be sued. Honey, your baby ass is headed for outer space because you don't have any real sources. You've been talking to some Wall Street flunkies who are jealous as hell of the brilliance of my fiance. Well, you know what? He also has brilliant lawyers who are gonna put nails in the coffin called your career for this libel! (*MONICA rises dramatically with her bottle, paces.*)

ANNIE. (*Approaching her.*) Monica, please. I don't think he would have come here tonight if he didn't have some kind of real sources!

MONICA. (*To Joel.*) Who are your federal sources? Who?! Names!

JOEL. You know I can't name names.

MONICA. You can't name names because you don't have anybody at the SEC! You don't have anybody at the U.S. Attorney's office! You don't have a fuckin' story! Your paper isn't running this story because they're not quite as wet behind the ears as you are!

ANNIE. Oh, Monica! He's just—a person!

IZZY. I'm sorry, Joel. I'm sorry she's like this. Christ!

MONICA. Can he go now? I really think it's past his bedtime.

JOEL. (*Picks up his suitcase, stands. Pause.*) I—I have something to say.

MONICA. If it's not a rock solid law enforcement source, don't waste your baby breath.

(*JOEL nods, opens his suitcase rigidly, determined to control his anger at all costs.*)

JOEL. (*Pulling out about five pictures.*) I uh—I brought along some pictures of Charles Stockwell accepting a briefcase of cash from a well-known trader in a dark alley in the middle of the night who has already been arrested by the Feds today. I'm sure you'll recognize the trader, and I'm sure he'll finger your fiance to save himself. (*HE holds them out to her.*)

MONICA. No newspaper on earth can do anything based on your personal photo album, darling. (*SHE grabs them, rifles through them.*)

JOEL. I took them early on in the investigation, I'm showing them to you in confidence because I can't name names to you, as you of all people know.

MONICA. (*Finishing her glance.*) So they're pictures of Chuck with a briefcase. Anything could be in that briefcase. Socks! Golf balls! Girl Scout cookies! You've got pictures of a briefcase, not money or a bribe, you fool! (*SHE hands them back to him like a slap in the face.*)

JOEL. (*HE takes them, puts them in his suitcase and closes it.*) I—I have something else to say.

IZZY. Joel?! If you want more abuse there's plenty of willing people on the street who will help you out!

MONICA. God! This is a torture!

JOEL. I—well, Monica—may I call you Monica?

MONICA. No! Call me Alice!

JOEL. I—well I—respect you very much. I do. Even though I—do not think you're being very polite, and there is no question that I have the Federal sources that you have accused me of not having, and there is no question that your fiance is a crook and will be arrested on Monday, I want you to know that I came here tonight against my better judgement as a favor to Isabelle because I respect you! I respect you and your show so much that you are one of the people who inspired me to go into this business in the first place! I think you have integrity as a reporter, and I think your sister does as well, and we knew we could tell you this and you would not warn your fiance to get outta town before the Feds nail him because you have too much integrity! And what I really want to say is—well, what I really want to say is, I hope when you calm down that you will see the light and save yourself from this—common criminal!

MONICA. Oh, my God, he's a yuppie with a Christ complex!

ANNIE. Monica, that's enough!

(MONICA goes to a counter, grabs a bottle and some car keys, goes to the door.)

ANNIE. Where you going?

MONICA. Driving. (To Joel, at the door.) One last thing. Are you fucking my sister as well?

IZZY. Oh, I just hate her guts!

MONICA. Thanks for the fuckin' wedding gift, Izzy! (*MONICA storms out to the street.*)

IZZY. (*Running to the door.*) Monica, you're still gonna have to deal with it!

ANNIE. Let her go, Izzy!

IZZY. What the hell else could we have done?

JOEL. Isabelle! You didn't—well, she doesn't have any reason to believe that you and I are—that way, does she?

IZZY. Forget it, Joel!

JOEL. I am certainly not who she thinks I am. I am most definitely not that kind of guy!

ANNIE. I'm dead on my feet, I'm passing out. Please, do not wake me if the house blows up!

IZZY. Annie?!

ANNIE. I am unconscious! (*ANNIE exits the back steps, upset. Pause.*)

IZZY. Shit! You think Annie is mad at me too?

JOEL. It's just—upsetting news no matter what. But we did do the only decent thing we could do.

IZZY. Damn! Life bites, it really does! (*IZZY puts out a cigarette, takes more of her drink.*)

JOEL. (*Rests his briefcase on the table, awkward.*) Isabelle, you didn't—break our little secret to Monica about how you rifled through Stockwell's drawers or anything, did you?

IZZY. God, no! Are you nuts?!

JOEL. Just remember that it needs to stay a secret. It gave us an important clue, but you know we're not using it because it is—illegal.

IZZY. I'm not stupid. What are you trying to say?

JOEL. Just be careful. I'm glad you did it because it pointed us in the right direction, but just remember that I didn't ask you to do it. I just don't want Monica to think I take pleasure in wrecking people's—personal relationships, that's all.

IZZY. Don't worry, she'll blame me forever for it. Shit! Why did I even participate in this fucking story. If I was sane I'd have run the other way, right?

JOEL. Now, Isabelle, it's too late for any of that.

IZZY. I'm sorry she—well you sure did stand up to her, though!

JOEL. Was I too disrespectful when I said she was impolite?

IZZY. Are you kidding? She treated you like you were a spittoon!

JOEL. You don't think she'll really go through with it now that she knows he's a total sleazeball, do you?

IZZY. Scumbag sleazeball toad!

JOEL. Will she?

IZZY. Who knows?

JOEL. Why would she? God, she's—well, she's got everything, I mean she's talented and successful and smart and—beautiful.

(Pause. IZZY reacts, awkward.)

JOEL. She's prettier in person than she is on TV. That happens with a lot of people, you know, it has to do with tape instead of film.

IZZY. Yeah, I know somethin' about it myself, I was a model.

JOEL. I know!

IZZY. It sucked.

JOEL. All I mean is that Monica could do a lot better than this guy. In the end she'll thank you. If we hadn't investigated this guy, somebody else would've nailed him later.

IZZY. "We"?!

JOEL. You deserve to have your name on this story.

IZZY. My name? You mean like a byline?!

JOEL. Yeah. I think this is a double byline story. Actually, I think I've just about convinced my editor to let you share the byline with me.

IZZY. Oh, my God! But—I'm just like a secretary!

JOEL. No. You're an editorial assistant who killed herself on a story for me and deserves credit for half the work. It's only fair.

IZZY. Oh, Jeez, what a time to be democratic!

JOEL. You thought I'd just take it away from you? I'd never do that.

IZZY. Why not?

JOEL. Well, because I—because it's just not right, that's all.

IZZY. Not because you like me?

JOEL. No!

IZZY. (*Disappointed.*) You don't like me?

JOEL. Of course I like you! I mean, I consider you a colleague and a friend.

IZZY. You really think I could make it as a reporter on my own?

JOEL. Absolutely! You certainly have the guts

IZZY. (*Pause.*) I guess I've always had guts. I had guts when I was a model, too, you know, even though I did it for my mother. She had guts in the end so I guess like mine are inherited. You know what I mean?

JOEL. No. Listen, Isabelle. I gotta get to a private phone.

IZZY. Did I tell you what happened to me when I was modelling?

JOEL. It's late. Maybe you could tell me another—

IZZY. See, I'd always hated how I felt when I had to walk or skip or jump down some goddamn runway to some ditzy music to please some son-of-a-bitch. This one time, see, at this big fall showing in Boston, I was wearing this ridiculous mink and halfway down the runway I got this idea—like a lightning bolt in my brain—that I should just rip it off and dance the way I wanted! Well, I ripped off the coat and threw it and before I knew it I'd ripped off the dress underneath and the underwear too! I was naked except for these heels, so I kicked those off and started to jump up and down on all fours, like a gorilla! I spotted this big fruit basket and I just started to gorge, I was spitting out cherry pits, peach pits, plum pits, you name it, I spit it! God, I was having such a good time! Well the music went screeching off, people ran, and the designer started screaming in my ear, "YOU FREAK! YOU ANIMAL! YOU FREAK!" when the security guards hauled me away. I just screamed back, "I AM A HUMAN BEING, DESCENDED FROM APES! DESCENDED FROM APES!"... Time to quit the biz, eh? You wanna go get a drink and figure out how to proceed with this damn story?

JOEL. I should probably get to that Inn.

IZZY. Oh, come on! I really just mean talk about the byline.

(Pause.)

JOEL. You mean after going out on a limb to see you get a well-deserved break you don't want it?

IZZY. Depends on how hard you wanna convince me.

(*A MAN appears on the porch. HE carries an overnight bag over his shoulder and a small shopping bag. HE stops on the porch, gathers his strength. JOEL and IZZY don't see him.*)

JOEL. Some things are just ethically right and that's why you do them, Isabelle. Did it ever occur to you that you make things far more complicated than they have to be?

IZZY. All the time, it runs in the family. Start talkin'. There's a bar just down the street.

JOEL. (*Going to the door.*) I really have to get back to the Inn and make this call.

(*The MAN walks to the screen door with resolve. It is ROGER. HE is handsome and has a kind of intense, driven energy.*)

IZZY. (*Sees him. Shocked.*) Roger!

ROGER. (*Opening the door.*) Isabelle. Is Monica here? I have to talk to her. I have to talk to her right away. (*Checks his watch.*) Sorry it's so late. I—I was in traffic, there was an accident.

IZZY. You drove here from Hartford?

ROGER. Uh-huh.

IZZY. Is she expecting you?

ROGER. I sincerely doubt it.

IZZY. (*Goes to the door, closes it behind him and then closes the door to the upstairs, so Annie won't hear.*) You want a drink? You look like you could use one.

ROGER. Just water. Thanks. (*Puts his bag on a chair.*)

(*IZZY closes a window, gets Roger water.*)

JOEL. (*Sticking his hand out.*) Joel Silverman, how do you do.

ROGER. (*Takes it, shakes absently.*) I've been better. Is she here?

IZZY. Uh—no.

JOEL. (*Pointing.*) She just went—

IZZY. (*Finishing.*) Out! She just went out, Joel. Far away. I mean, across town, Roger. To see Chuck. That's the guy she's marrying tomorrow. You do know she's getting married tomorrow?

ROGER. Uh-huh. Read it.

IZZY. Joel, this is Roger. Roger Dowling? The man I mentioned to you, the one who Monica lived with for two years before Chuck? (*IZZY hands the water to Roger.*)

(*HE takes it, drinks, holds the bag in the other hand.*)

JOEL. Ah! Oh. Well then why don't you have a seat, Robert.

IZZY. (*Correcting.*) Roger!

ROGER. I just have to talk to Monica. Can I wait for her here?

(*JOEL sits, fascinated.*)

IZZY. Uh—no.

ROGER. She tell you to say that if I showed up?

IZZY. No.

ROGER. Then I'll wait. (*HE sits. Pause.*)

IZZY. (*Indicating the bag.*) That a wedding present?

ROGER. Not exactly.

IZZY. It's not exactly but kind of a wedding present?

ROGER. Isabelle, can I be frank?

JOEL. (*Over anxious.*) Please!

ROGER. Who is this guy?

IZZY. A friend, never mind him. I mean you can talk in front of him, he's nobody.

JOEL. Thanks.

ROGER. She doesn't even know this guy Stockwell. I know you don't know me very well, we only met once, but if I could tell you the shit I have been through with that woman, your sister, who you know is not an easy person, you would understand why, when I read in some goddamn society column that she was marrying some fucking power-monger who she's known for only three measly months, I was overwhelmed with the desire to wring her little neck!

IZZY. You came here to wring her little neck?

ROGER. I got over it.

IZZY. Good thinking.

JOEL. (*To Izzy.*) Your sister sure knows how to pick 'em.

ROGER. (*To Joel.*) I'm not in the mood, bud, okay?

JOEL. Fine.

(*Pause.*)

IZZY. (*Sitting by him.*) Roger. Listen, Roger. We're glad you're here. We're very glad you came.

(*JOEL gives her a look.*)

ROGER. Then lemme talk to her.

IZZY. She's really not here. She's really out, and—and—well, Roger, I don't exactly think you're in the right frame of mind to talk to her, I mean wouldn't you say you're a little worked up?

ROGER. Maybe. Hard drive.

IZZY. And—well, the truth of it, you see, is that she just got some very bad news about Chuck, so she's a little—worked up herself. You put worked up and worked up together and—one of the neighbors might end up calling the cops if things get loud and—someone might wind up in a local emergency room where they're kinda—low on staff! That might be be something you'd like to avoid at this time.

ROGER. What bad news.

IZZY. Oh, it's nothing, it's just—well, he's a criminal.

ROGER. You're kidding!

JOEL. (*To Izzy.*) Nothing?! A few seconds ago he was a scumbag sleazeball—

IZZY. (*Cutting him off.*) Joel!

ROGER. (*Delighted.*) I can't believe it! Wait a minute. It makes perfect sense. I should've guessed it! Embezzling?

IZZY. Pay-offs of millions, you know, it could be a lot worse.

ROGER. So she's cancelling the ceremony anyway?

IZZY. She's hangin' on like a dog with a bone.

ROGER. She does that.

IZZY. Some people find it impressive.

ROGER. The woman is a ballbuster. Spends her whole life trying to get back at her father. I wish to God she could just believe that I am not gonna turn into that son of a bitch!

IZZY. Word of advice? Don't say things like you're gonna wring her little neck.

(Pause.)

ROGER. I am worked up, I'm sorry.

IZZY. Why don't you tell me what you came to say to her. Rehearse it, you know. Maybe I could help out or something.

ROGER. It's between she and I. I mean—her and me. What time's the ceremony.

IZZY. Three o'clock.

ROGER. *(Rising.)* I'll come back in the morning. I'll be calm then. I'll be back here first thing in the morning.

IZZY. You can stay where Joel's staying, it's this place just down the street!

ROGER. Fine.

IZZY. Joel?

JOEL. I'm supposed to take him to the Inn? What fun.

IZZY. You said you were going anyway.

JOEL. We were gonna have a drink.

IZZY. *(With an exasperated cry.)* Oh! I'll take you, Roger. Then we'll have that drink you were just dyin' to have a few minutes ago, Joel. Only you're paying!

JOEL. Fine.

IZZY. Uh—Roger?

(ROGER stops.)

IZZY. Could you at least tell me what's in the bag?

ROGER. (*Pause. Hands it to Izzy.*) Her diary. She moves out on me one day with no warning after I have asked her, I have pleaded with her to please not move out on me ever until we have agreed that that's it, we can't make it. I mean we even went to this couples doctor together, she knew how I felt about it. I had two mothers die on me, you know? I have my own problems with being left. So what does she do? She moves out on me because I didn't show up at her birthday party because she didn't think it was important enough for her to come to a public health benefit that it took me months to set up. Of course it wasn't important enough. Nothing I did was ever that important to her. Okay, so I shoulda gone to her party anyway. I wasn't big enough, I was pissed. She still didn't have to move out and refuse to speak to me. If she really never wanted to see me again, she wouldn't have left this diary. You don't leave a diary behind unless you're still trying to get through to somebody in a totally ass backwards way, right?

IZZY. (*Pulls it out of the bag as he talks, examines it. It is a book but it is all taped up with masking tape.*) Why's there tape on it?

ROGER. (*Shrugs.*) I taped it shut.

IZZY. Huh?

ROGER. I taped it shut. I didn't read it, I didn't even wanna be tempted to read it. I'm not gonna play her little games anymore. Give it to her. Tell her I didn't read it and I want her to say whatever the hell she was trying to say to me by leaving it behind to my face.

IZZY. (*Stunned.*) How could you restrain yourself?!

ROGER. I'm not playing anymore, it's gotten us nowhere.

IZZY. (*Putting it in the bag.*) I'll make sure she gets it! Boy, will I make sure! Keep your voice down as you go out, there's people sleeping and the windows are open.

ROGER. Okay.

(*ROGER exits first, followed by IZZY and then JOEL, who shakes his head at Izzy. ROGER disappears ahead of the other two, in the opposite direction from where the tent is.*)

JOEL. If she would only get to know me.

IZZY. Shut up, Joel. Just shut up!

(*JOEL exits the back door across the porch and disappears, after ROGER, just as ANNIE calls from the top of the steps.*)

ANNIE. (*Offstage.*) Izzy? Izzy!

(*IZZY freezes, hides the diary on her person and stuffs the bag in a drawer.*)

IZZY. (*Calling after Joel, definitively.*) Go ahead without me! I'll follow! Gimme a minute alone!

ANNIE. (*Appears from the backstage in her robe. SHE looks like she's been at least trying to sleep.*) Did I hear a man's voice?

IZZY. Well—Joel is a man even though Monica just bit his dick off!

ANNIE. Are you headed out?

IZZY. I'm just taking him to the Inn, I'll be right back, I swear! You don't think Monica went to warn Chuck, do you? She promised she wouldn't!

ANNIE. She'll keep her promise.

IZZY. I'm sorry, Annie. I'm really sorry I'm not together like you.

ANNIE. Don't apologize, you haven't done anything wrong.

IZZY. I'm not always gonna be a fuck up, you know. Some people think I can change!

ANNIE. You did not fuck up! Now get going so you can get back here and get into bed!

IZZY. Thank you, Annie. You're the only one who ever made me feel like—well, like you were glad I was alive.

ANNIE. (*Pause.*) Would you get your little butt down that street?

(*IZZY nods, goes out. Pause. ANNIE looks after her, sadly, then gets some milk from the fridge and pours it into a pan to heat it. A moment passes and a CAR pulls up. It is MONICA. SHE slams the door and appears, very bedraggled, with her empty bottle. SHE looks in at Annie, in much the same way as Izzy did just before.*)

MONICA. Is she upstairs?

ANNIE. She's out.

MONICA. Good. I hate her! I hate her, she hates me. After all the time and—work I've put into understanding my family, I have a sister who still hates me! (*SHE starts to cry.*) Do you still hate me too?

ANNIE. Oh, God, Monica! Come in here! (*ANNIE gently kind of pulls Monica into the room.*)

MONICA. You do, don't you?

ANNIE. Of course not!

MONICA. Well I hate her anyway!

ANNIE. You do not!

MONICA. Oh, just let me say it! (*MONICA blows her nose into her sleeve.*)

(*ANNIE laughs, MONICA follows, dries her eyes.*)

ANNIE. Where'd you go?

MONICA. Nowhere. Just drove around by myself.

ANNIE. You want some—hot milk or tea or coffee or something?

MONICA. Tea would be nice.

ANNIE. Okay.

(*MONICA sits, pooped. ANNIE takes her milk off the stove, puts on water, gets tea, cups, spoons.*)

MONICA. (*Tries to get a nonexistent last sip from her bottle, seeing herself.*) God! Look at this! Did I drink that? I couldn't have, I don't drink!

ANNIE. (*Picking up on it, as if different people are talking.*) "No, thank you, I don't drink." "What a coincidence, I don't drink either." "You don't? Well then let's have a drink. Scotch and soda?" "Skip the soda." "Perrr-fect." (*ANNIE stops, looks at Monica with a meaningful twinkle.*)

MONICA. Schizophrenia or one of your talking sculptures?

ANNIE. The latter. One in the new series entitled, "Do as I say, not as I do."

MONICA. I don't drink, I really don't!

ANNIE. I'm just telling you about a sculpture.

MONICA. Why the hell didn't Izzy tell me earlier?!

ANNIE. They just yesterday put all the pieces together, I swear!

MONICA. It's gotta be that damn crib incident! I took that pillow and I smushed it right into her little wrinkled face! God, what was I thinking?!

ANNIE. (*Amused.*) You know I was looking at Izzy before and I was remembering—just because of the odd way she was standing—that time that her arm fell out of the socket and just hung there funny, you know, swingin' back and forth like it was dead when she moved. (*ANNIE imitates.*)

MONICA. (*Laughing.*) Gross! Why do you have to remember such a gross thing? Stop it!

ANNIE. It was weird. It went right back in though, I just popped it right back in 'cause I didn't know what else to do and it worked.

MONICA. Did I pull it out? Don't tell me if I did!

ANNIE. No! You didn't.

MONICA. How did it happen?

ANNIE. How do you think.

(*Pause.*)

MONICA. I don't know how you can stand to remember everything.

ANNIE. It happened in the car, after he put Mom in the hospital with the broken jaw and the bleeding.

MONICA. Oh, God, I remember that! Her jaw was wired shut when he took us to see her and she kept saying, (*As if her jaw is wired shut:*) I love you kids! Don't forget I love you kids! I love you kids!

ANNIE. (*With a laugh.*) Right! Yes! She kept saying that.

MONICA. Oh, God, then he shuffled us all out of the hospital and took us to Church to pray for OUR sins! Izzy wailed all the way from the hospital—she wouldn't get out of the car so he pulled her by the arm from the back into the front. ... Annie, how do you explain my instinct to kill her and yours to save her.

ANNIE. I'm a better person.

MONICA. (*Whines.*) Don't say that! You don't have to say it, do you?

ANNIE. Just cut it with the guilt!

MONICA. (*Self-mocking.*) How can I? It's such an integral part of my life! (*Pause.*) So why the hell don't you hate me?

ANNIE. Because I did and I got over it!

MONICA. You did hate me?!

ANNIE. Monica, would you please?

MONICA. I am sorry I'm such a bitch! You know, it helps though, being a bitch sometimes. I mean, I wouldn't have gotten my own talk show if I wasn't a bitch. Besides, it would make me very happy to just once hear someone— i.e., a man—define "bitch." I ask my producer, my cameramen, my male staff members all the time to just give me a real honest to God definition and they can't! They say, "A bitch is a bitch. You just know a bitch when you see one." Well, I don't accept that! They can't define it because what bitch really means is a driven and in command woman. My producer comes into that studio like a wild bull 'cause somebody fucked up, and everybody goes, "Whoa, look at that Ralph, what a man!, some day he's gonna run the network." I come into that studio with a faint trace of smoke comin' outta one nostril 'cause one of my staff flat out gave me the wrong info and everybody goes, "Whoa, look out, the bitch is raggin' out again!" I tell you, Annie, it is a battlefield out there, we're all wearing Armani but the sexes are simply not from the same planet and together we have a national epidemic of total misunderstanding. (*SHE sighs, exhausted.*) Still, I'm sorry if to you I acted like a—well, like a bitch.

ANNIE. Monica, what the hell are you gonna do about Chuck.

MONICA. Kill him.

ANNIE. Before that, I've been thinking. Despite what you promised, I think you're gonna have to just tell Chuck you know.

MONICA. About what?

ANNIE. The investigation, the bribes, the whole deal! Jesus!

MONICA. I'm not a cop!

ANNIE. What if he goes to jail?!

MONICA. Oh, he won't go to jail! He can pay for the best lawyers in the business.

ANNIE. Don't you care that you can't trust this man?

MONICA. It's safe to say that it irks me a little.

ANNIE. MONICA! What are you gonna do?!

MONICA. Oh, Annie, for Christ's sakes what do you want me to say? I don't know! Why won't you talk to Harry?

ANNIE. Harry?!

MONICA. I'm thinking, I'm thinking! I need to focus my mind on something more hopeful for a few seconds!

ANNIE. (*Pause.*) Wouldn't it be kinda like—suicide for me to trust Harry again? Forgive the expression.

MONICA. No! He made one mistake, that's different from someone who makes a million. Believe me, he's sorry.

ANNIE. (*Pours the water for the tea and brings it over, sits.*) How do I know he won't do it again?

MONICA. You never know that, that's life! He told me one day when I was buying up a storm in one of his stores that you were the only woman he ever wanted to marry!

ANNIE. He said that?!

MONICA. Yes!

ANNIE. Well, no wonder he had to betray me. He wanted me too much!

MONICA. Annie, he was young! He was young and stupid and you were too hurt to do anything but—test him every step of the way!

ANNIE. Not every step of the way!

MONICA. Those are your words!

ANNIE. I exaggerated, it was every other step!

MONICA. You were engaged and you were always daring him to go out with other women!

ANNIE. (*Ironic.*) Are you suggesting I have a trust problem? Why, I never once thought of it that way.

MONICA. Then after Mom's death, when you finally deemed it permissible for you and I to become friends—

thank God—you told me you started to think about Harry constantly.

ANNIE. Then. Thought about. Past tense.

MONICA. Well here he is, marry him! You can borrow my dress!

ANNIE. It's all right for me to marry a caterer, but it sure as hell wouldn't be all right for you!

MONICA. The caterer isn't in love with me!

ANNIE. (*Blurts.*) Neither is the investment banker-crook!

(ANNIE gasps, hearing herself and MONICA stops as if slapped, looks away, shaken. Sincere:)

ANNIE. Oh, I didn't mean that! I meant—shit, Monica, I meant it the other way around, I meant—well you're not ... I'm sorry.

MONICA. You're right, don't be sorry! Of course I love him, but I'm not IN love with him! In love is for kids, I'm thirty-three years old, I love him maturely, as it should be. Sometimes I think he's silly enough to—entertain a few thoughts about being in love with me when we're out with fancy and important people, you know, when I look great and I'm playing perfect and together Monica the talk show queen to the hilt. I am a good package, after all. You might be wrong although I'm not entirely sure.

ANNIE. Of course I'm wrong! I said it backwards!

MONICA. He wants my children!

ANNIE. Do you want your kids to have to visit their Daddy in jail?

MONICA. He's not going to jail on me, that bastard!

ANNIE. Maybe if you—called him and told him about the investigation he would volunteer to confess before they nail him!

MONICA. Better yet, maybe Izzy and Joel could just—drop it! What about giving them money?

ANNIE. You mean a bribe?!

MONICA. No, I mean giving them money to forget it!

ANNIE. That's a bribe!

MONICA. Fine. Be technical at a time like this.

ANNIE. It's completely irrational!

MONICA. It's insane! What am I saying, I'm in the news business!

ANNIE. Don't marry him, Monica!

MONICA. He's not even a particularly nice person, I don't even like him!

ANNIE. (*Letting go.*) For God's sake, get on that phone right this minute and put this wedding off!

MONICA. I have to go through with it!

ANNIE. You do not!

MONICA. I do!

ANNIE. WHY?

MONICA. (*Desperate.*) Because I—because I—because I always wanted to have a baby with a trust fund!

ANNIE. What?

MONICA. A trust fund! If I'm married to Chuck my children will be born with trust funds! They'll be secure, they'll never have to worry! They won't be—tossed into the world without something to cling to like we were!

ANNIE. How can you say that after all the suffering you've had? It wasn't lack of money!

MONICA. We weren't rich, all my friends had sailboats and extra shoes!

ANNIE. You had extra shoes! Me and Izzy didn't get any!

MONICA. Cecily Hill always had—pastel shoes! I remember this one pair she had, oo, I coulda just ripped her feet off for 'em. They were pink with precious little white bows on the front!

ANNIE. Who would wear shoes like that?

MONICA. I happen to own several pairs, different shades of pink.

ANNIE. Excuuuse me! (*Pause.*) If you'd had pastel shoes Krazy-glued to your feet throughout your childhood you still woulda been in the same sinkin' boat with the rest of us.

MONICA. My baby is gonna have a trust fund if it's the last goddamn thing I do. If you can't get the love I say go for the bucks.

ANNIE. What baby?

(*Pause.*)

MONICA. When I have a baby, whenever. (*MONICA gets up, uncomfortable, gets herself water from the sink and drinks.*) God, what a headache! There's a little man with a crowbar inside my ear trying to move my brain to the left.

ANNIE. Monica, are you ... Are you? (*Pause.*) No!

MONICA. You'll be an aunt, won't that be nice?!

ANNIE. Oh my God!

MONICA. Remain calm. I might've just bombed it out with alcohol anyway.

ANNIE. Monica, how could you?!

MONICA. I'm thirty-three years old, Annie, what am I waiting for? Chuck is dying for this baby!

ANNIE. So you're having a baby for Chuck?!

MONICA. I can't have an abortion, Annie. If I do there's no guarantee I'll ever conceive again and I want a family. I want a family more than I ever wanted my career, and I'm gonna get one. Goddamn it, I'm gonna get one somehow!

ANNIE. You can have the baby and—marry someone you love! Maybe after like a rest you could go back at it with Roger!

MONICA. Roger?! You don't even know Roger, you stayed with us for one weekend and you keep trying to push me back together with Roger? Why?

ANNIE. Well, what happened, Monica? After two years of a relationship with a man you told me you loved, you move out one day and that's it?! He seemed like a person with integrity to me, isn't he?

MONICA. All we do is fight.

ANNIE. Did he—he didn't—I mean he wouldn't—

MONICA. (*Cutting her off.*) Of course not!

(*Pause.*)

ANNIE. He must love you a lot to have kept—trying to make the relationship work!

MONICA. Oh, Annie, he's got this dread fear of abandonment, I mean let me tell you, it is a big fucking drag to have to deal with! His mother was killed in a car crash when he was seven and then his stepmother was killed in a plane crash when he was thirteen and he won't go to therapy himself to deal with that because he says it's too painful, but he wants me to keep going to deal with what I find too painful? Now is that fair?!

ANNIE. Tell him you'll stay out of cars and planes.

(MONICA gives her a look.)

ANNIE. No, it's not fair.

MONICA. Him and his goddamn public health work. Why can't he just be a money-grubbing M.D. like everybody else!

ANNIE. Oh, Monica, that wouldn't solve the problem, would it?

MONICA. No. But even when we do talk about marriage, he says we shouldn't have children for another two or three years! Can you believe that? Two or three years?! My tongue is hanging out! He knows I want one now, so he just dangles it in front of me forever like a carrot!

ANNIE. How about going back to therapy, Monica? I mean just for yourself, never mind him.

MONICA. That'll be my eighth therapist, Annie! Number eight!

ANNIE. So?

MONICA. It's humiliating! Just—being in therapy endlessly doesn't turn you into somebody else, believe me, I know because I tried! I don't seem to get better, Annie. In some ways I only—feel more pain. ... Why are you trying to help me so much?!

ANNIE. *(Ironic.)* Because I hate you!

MONICA. Stop! *(MONICA moves away, awkward. Tries to pull herself together.)* I still think I can make this marriage to Chuck work. I just have to get on that phone, give him the bad news without naming names, after he promises to keep his ass in town, and tell him that over my dead body is my child going to have to visit her scumbag criminal Daddy in jail, trust fund or no trust fund. (*SHE marches to the phone.*)

ANNIE. Don't you think you should deliver this kind of news in person?

MONICA. (*Dialing the phone.*) Yes! I'll tell him I'm coming over! Then if he promises not to break the law anymore and go clean, once this mess is behind us, we'll be fine. (*Into the phone:*) Chuck? Chuck did I wake you? ... Well you don't have to curse, Chuck, I wouldn't be calling at this hour unless it was urgent. ... I have something very pressing to discuss with you before we get married tomorrow. Can I come over? ... Well can you come over here? ... I don't wanna say what it's about over the phone. ... No, it is not about the baby, the baby is fine. ... I wouldn't lie to you about the baby, Chuck. ... Yes, I understand that the baby is the priority here, but you don't have to keep saying it, do you? ... Thanks. I'm on my way. (*SHE hangs up, sighs. Pause.*) Well. This seems right.

(*ANNIE stares.*)

MONICA. What?

ANNIE. Does he always—talk to you like that?

MONICA. (*Getting her bag, her keys.*) Oh, he's tired, it's not what it sounds like. Don't assume you know from one incident.

ANNIE. That's one of my subtitles in the new series. Mom used to say that a lot.

MONICA. Oh, for Christ's sakes, Annie, you're way too sensitive, never mind idealistic!

(Pause.)

ANNIE. I am. You're right.

MONICA. I gotta get over there, I gotta go. (*MONICA goes to the door, stops, comes back a bit.*) Life is full of compromises, Annie. He's gonna love this baby like crazy because he wants it.

ANNIE. A lot of people would want your baby, Monica.

MONICA. To hell with a lot of people! This one's here, ready, and despite this unfortunate bullshit I know he will never turn into him! Never!

ANNIE. You mean he'd never hurt you.

(Pause.)

MONICA. After he'd level Mom he'd always tell me it was my fault. Every time he hit her I felt guilty that he wasn't hitting me.

ANNIE. He was hitting all of us.

MONICA. (*Almost whispers.*) I thought one day he'd just kill me.

ANNIE. He was an alcoholic, he was mentally ill.

MONICA. He was a sadist.

ANNIE. It's over.

(Pause.)

MONICA. You're right. Time to let it the hell go. I'm gonna marry Chuck and forget it. Mom loved us. I think I really, really know that Mom in her way loved us.

(ANNIE nods. Pause.)

MONICA. Sometimes on the show when I'm armed with the microphone and I'm talking to these reformed guys—you know, a rapist, a drug dealer, a murderer who's found God or re-hab, this—person starts rearin' up inside of me. I like to think of her as—Rambo Monica. The public defender, the seeker of revenge and justice? (*Demonstrating with a "microphone," circling Annie and shoving it back and forth at her as if she's a "guest" on the show:*) "Do you know you've ruined lives?!" ... "Do you know you've scarred people?!" ... "Do you know your victim will never trust another human being again?!" ... "Do you know if I really shove this microphone at you I'm gonna be nationally humiliated and then fired?!"

ANNIE. (*Amused.*) God, that must be awful!

MONICA. Oh, no. No, no. I'm a pro, I'm a pro. I just check that little impulse, stick it in my kidneys. (*Pause.*) Annie, didn't you ever wanna just ask him why he had to be so mean to us?

ANNIE. I did ask him.

MONICA. You didn't!

ANNIE. Yes I did.

MONICA. To his face?!

ANNIE. Uh-huh.

MONICA. Was he sober?

ANNIE. Uh-huh.

MONICA. What did he say?

ANNIE. He said he didn't know. He said he really had no idea.

(Pause.)

MONICA. I gotta get goin', I gotta get the hell over there and tell Chuck. I think I need a jacket. Don't you think it's colder out there, don't I need a jacket?

ANNIE. I'll get you one, I'll be right down. (*ANNIE exits up steps.*)

MONICA. (*Still pacing, circling the empty chair for a moment; using the "microphone" as if her father was in the chair, but her tone is different, soft, sweet:*) Was it me who made you so unhappy? (*Moving, almost shy with microphone.*) Could I have done anything to fix it? (*And again.*) Could I have cured you, Daddy? (*And again.*) If I could have I would've done anything to—cure you. (*SHE sits, exhausted.*

ANNIE. (*Re-enters with a jacket.*) Here you go!

MONICA. (*Putting on jacket.*) Thanks. I—well you know how I feel about you.

ANNIE. Wake me if you want when you get back.

MONICA. Sweet—well, sweet dreams, anyway.

ANNIE. Thanks.

(MONICA exits porch. ANNIE goes to the door and watches as LIGHTS fade.)

End Scene Two

End Act I

ACT II

LIGHTS go up on the kitchen, the following day, at about noon. ANNIE, wearing her robe and filing her nails, sits tensely at the kitchen table with PAT, sipping coffee and having a little breakfast. PAT is already dressed and adds on a calculator.

ANNIE. I can't believe she'd still go through with it.

PAT. The thing is, after the trial, exactly how much is he gonna be worth. Even if he fully cooperates with the government, the net worth is gonna suffer. I mean we need figures.

ANNIE. I guess she didn't wake me 'cause she didn't wanna listen to me.

PAT. All she wanted was sleeping pills and reassurance. But like I told her, she's gotta sit him right down at that table with a calculator and make sure he'll still be worth it financially.

ANNIE. Do you have to be so—cold and calculating?

PAT. I am cold and calculating.

ANNIE. Oh, it was five o'clock in the morning, right? She didn't know what she was saying.

PAT. She struck me as completely rational, despite the fact that she looked like a corpse. Poor girl. Does not deserve this shit. She did say though that Chuck annoyed her less than usual when confronted with this crisis. Acted like a man.

ANNIE. You said she told you he broke down and wept.

PAT. Men are allowed to cry too, Annie. That's what they call societal progress.

ANNIE. Did you hear Izzy come in?

PAT. About an hour before Monica.

ANNIE. Shit.

PAT. Kid or no kid, what's the use if he's gonna lose all his millions? Couldn't she find herself a huckster who's smart enough to not get caught?

ANNIE. Don't you think Monica deserves more even if he keeps his damn millions?!

PAT. Sure. We all deserve more. Adulthood is about deserving more and settling for less. It's the illusions that nail you in life, not the reality! One of your illusions is that married people are supposed to have some kinda deep and profound love between them that few people in life ever attain. Did it ever occur to you that many of us know we're not up to it and so are relieved to settle for just getting by with an approximation?

ANNIE. Oh, I don't think I can do that!

PAT. So don't. Now there's always the movies too. I mean, if the trial does drag on for months and Chuck's gotta fork over most of his millions—the worst scenario—then he could still write a best-selling book and—

ANNIE. (*Jumping up, getting more coffee.*) Pat! I can't believe that most people truthfully accept living without any spark, any—passion in their marriages!

PAT. I do, and I don't miss it a bit. It was never there. Now how can we figure out exactly how much he's gonna lose? I got it! I'll call my lawyer! (*SHE gets up, goes to phone.*)

ANNIE. Pat! Please! Maybe we should just wake Monica up now and—

(As PAT reaches the phone the door to the steps opens and MONICA enters, frantic. SHE has thrown on her wedding dress without buttoning it; SHE looks confused and carries a make-up case.)

MONICA. What time is it, is it two already?
ANNIE. Monica!
PAT. Noon, you got three hours!
MONICA. *(With a huge sigh of relief.)* Oh my God.

(SHE collapses in a chair. PAT gets her water.)

MONICA. Thank God. The clock upstairs is wrong, I thought it was two.
ANNIE. Are you all right?
MONICA. No, I thought it was two. I need a full hour for make-up, this goddamn thing's being filmed and everything. Has the crew arrived? Are the cameras set up?
PAT. There's enough equipment out there to broadcast live to Tasmania. *(PAT hands her the water.)*
MONICA. Thanks.

(SHE drinks, PAT sits.)

MONICA. Well, I had to have film, I did not want tape. Tape flattens you out, makes you look like a leftover pancake. I must be lit right. You know one reason Ba-Ba Wa-Wa looks so good is she's always lit right.
PAT. Another is that everything on that face has been moved up, around and over.

MONICA. The lighting must be checked, Pat. Everything must be checked.

PAT. Everything will be checked, honey. That's what I'm here for.

MONICA. God, I dreamt that I missed the ceremony and it took place without me anyway. Can you imagine? Chuck was marrying Brenda Starr—you know, that doll that I had as a kid? She was great as a doll but boy did she look like shit! Her hair was wrong, her dress was downright ugly and her shoes were this ridiculous shade of—skip the shoes. I woke up sick to my stomach, even my subconscious is after me. (*SHE drinks more.*) Now Annie, everything has been worked out very nicely with Chuck, I just didn't get much sleep so I'm a little wired. He called his lawyer right away, agreed to co-operate fully with the U.S. government, didn't turn any blame on me, get that—no blame on me—and took full responsibility for the mistake right away.

ANNIE. Good.

MONICA. Good?! It was great! He cried and everything, apologized. It was a little sickening to see his face turn all pink and puffy, but he was very sincere! He fell into the whole scam, he was not the one who went looking for trouble, as I suspected.

ANNIE. I'll bet.

MONICA. It's true! It was like a one-shot deal, a business partner told him there was this opportunity to make a killing and he took it because you wanna know why?

ANNIE. Not particularly.

MONICA. Me! I wanted this goddamn huge rock to wave in people's faces—and believe me, it did cost a fortune—so he did it specifically to buy it for me! I mean that means he must love me in his way because that makes it my fault but he's not blaming me! Can you believe it?

(ANNIE groans.)

PAT. How do you feel about having to hock it for groceries?

MONICA. Annie! Annie, isn't that kinda touching?

ANNIE. No.

MONICA. Well, it is! It is touching and I really need your support. He is completely committed to creating the image of a happy family!

ANNIE. The image! The goddamn image! What about the reality of lying in bed next to someone who's as cold as a gravestone?! How is that gonna make you feel?

MONICA. Safe. Something I plan on growing very fond of.

ANNIE. Bullshit! *(ANNIE gets up, gets more coffee. To Monica:)* Would you like some coffee?

MONICA. *(Shaking her head.)* I'll explode.

PAT. Listen. Monica. How much is he gonna lose.

MONICA. What?

PAT. Monica honey, I thought you were marrying Chuck for his—well I thought one of the main attractions about Chuck was his rather sizable net worth.

MONICA. ONE of the attractions.

PAT. Now we've really got a problem.

MONICA. He has a brilliant mind for finance, he'll find other ways to make back the millions. Besides, I make enough money to live very nicely!

PAT. (*Rising, troubled.*) I think I'll call my lawyer anyway. Maybe if you could look at some figures, you'd see things more clearly.

ANNIE. Pat!

PAT. I'll be upstairs on the phone. Don't move. (*PAT exits up the stairs.*)

MONICA. I need your support today, Annie. I really, really do.

ANNIE. Maybe I don't know what I'm talking about, maybe I am so idealistic that I'll live my whole life alone and end up one of those weird old ladies who only has conversations with small children and violets, but Monica, the image of a father and husband who impresses the neighbors is not gonna make you happy.

MONICA. That's silly. I'm not trying to be happy.

ANNIE. Well what do you imagine you'll be with Chuck in five or ten years?

MONICA. Middle-aged.

ANNIE. Miserable!

MONICA. I will be living a normal grown-up's life, somewhere in that vast middle ground between despair and hope. It won't be emotionally extreme in any direction, it will just be—limited. Like life is to grown ups. Limited.

ANNIE. That's your idea of a grown-up's life.

(*IZZY enters from the stairs, holding her head. SHE just got up. SHE wears a jacket with a big pocket. The diary is in the pocket, unseen.*)

IZZY. (*With a groan.*) There's no way I can manage this headache, no fuckin' way. I'm really sorry, Monica. Really, really sorry.

MONICA. (*Rising.*) You want aspirin or Tylenol? (*SHE goes happily to a drawer.*)

IZZY. (*Stares.*) You're not still mad at me?

MONICA. (*Pulling out both.*) For what? (*Pause. MONICA puts the pills down in front of Izzy, goes to the fridge.*) Juice?

IZZY. Please. (*To Annie, amazed:*) What happened?

ANNIE. Monica told Chuck and he's pleading guilty, cooperating with the government. In her mind everything is fine.

IZZY. Did you cancel the wedding?

MONICA. Of course not! (*Pause. MONICA puts the juice in front of her.*) Why would I go and do an impulsive thing like that?

IZZY. God, my head is splitting! (*IZZY takes some pills with the juice.*) What time is it? Has anybody else shown up yet? I mean—has anything else happened?

MONICA. Who would show up?

IZZY. (*Shrugs.*) Joel.

MONICA. I see absolutely no reason for that—child to come back here for one second. As it turns out, his little story is of no consequence anyway.

IZZY. (*To Annie.*) How could she say that?

ANNIE. She thinks she knows what she's doing.

(*MONICA gives her a look.*)

ANNIE. Maybe she does. Maybe for her it's—the right choice.

IZZY. I'm gone for ten minutes, you side with her.

ANNIE. It wasn't exactly ten minutes!

MONICA. (*Going to the stairs.*) I'm heading up to finish the make-up job. Boy, sometimes right before you start all those layers you think, who the hell invented make-up anyway? What is all this shit about, it's so—stupid and pointless. Then you smush it on your face and you realize how much better you look as somebody else.

IZZY. (*Incredulous.*) Monica?!

MONICA. (*Stopping.*) Not now, Izzy.

IZZY. Monica, at Mom's funeral we had a conversation!

MONICA. We did? How unusual.

IZZY. You said—and I remember it because I agreed with you, and it surprised me to hear it coming out of your mouth—

MONICA. Oh, I really don't need to hear another free-wheeling interpretation of reality from her!

IZZY. You said that what made you really sad about Mom and Dad—I mean, really, really sad, is that they showed us something ugly—something truly ugly between men and women that you would never wanna pass on to a child.

MONICA. I don't know why you're bringing this up. There is none of that between me and Chuck, it is not even relevant! Besides, all that has to exist between parents for a child to be well-adjusted is respect, which Chuck and I have! I interview experts on a daily basis. (*To Annie, meaning the baby.*) Does she know?

ANNIE. No.

IZZY. Know what?

ANNIE. In a second!

IZZY. Monica, you said you wanted to have kids with Roger!

MONICA. (*Losing it slightly at the mention of Roger.*)
I do not want you to speak to me anymore about Roger!

IZZY. Don't you wanna talk to him? I mean—if you
could, in your very well-concealed heart, wouldn't you
rather work it out with him?

MONICA. No! Absolutely not! It is completely over!
You haven't been in contact with him, have you?

IZZY. Uh-uh.

MONICA. You better not! I have nothing to say to
him, nothing!

IZZY. Why the fuck not?

MONICA. Because he has no right to be the father of
my children, no right because if he doesn't accept me as I
am, how can he accept my child?

IZZY. You and your child are not gonna be the same
person, Monica. (*Pause.*) What child?

MONICA. Look. Roger and I do not trust each other,
that's gotta mean we don't really love each other, right?
Chuck accepts me. He knows what he sees is what he gets,
and it's good enough for him. Now I'm going up!

IZZY. Monica!

MONICA. That's it! (*MONICA exits up the steps,
slams the door behind her.*)

(*IZZY collapses, drinks coffee.*)

ANNIE. This is like a fuckin' war zone here today.
Maybe it'll just never be any different.

IZZY. Annie! You cannot believe the night I had!

ANNIE. Maybe you should keep it to yourself.

IZZY. Monica is a lot more screwed up than I thought
she was! I mean, I have always known that underneath all

that fancy bullshit she's scared shitless of men, but—I didn't think it was this bad! I mean, I've been trying to stay away from boys because five seconds into a relationship and I'm obsessed and crazy and dangerous to the general public, but she gets in deep and then blows it sky high!

ANNIE. I give up! Maybe it is better to have a guy who looks the part, a guy you can live with instead of silence. ... What the hell do we know anyway? I avoid human beings when I don't even want to, and you—you run out and sleep with someone who's supposed to be your colleague!

IZZY. I did not sleep with him!

ANNIE. You telling me the truth?

IZZY. Yes!

(Pause.)

ANNIE. Just because I know it's really important to you that these people at the paper take you seriously, you don't wanna make that kinda thing a habit like—like you used to.

IZZY. When Joel could get his mind off Monica's love life long enough we argued about the damn double byline.

ANNIE. You're getting a byline?

IZZY. I'll find out today. Looks that way. You know, with his name too.

ANNIE. Isn't that terrific?

IZZY. Life just sucks. I finally bust my ass in a real job, use my brain, act like a grown up, and like— accomplish something only—let's face it, Annie. I wouldn't have busted my ass if I wasn't so fuckin' jealous of her.

ANNIE. Oh—so what? The guy's a crook whether your name's on the story or not! Don't you feel a sense of accomplishment?

IZZY. Yeah ...

ANNIE. Don't you feel like you could work that hard again to investigate someone who wasn't involved with Monica?

IZZY. I sure hope so.

ANNIE. Izzy, you will. This is great! So accept it as a well-deserved career break. Besides, look at this way. Monica doesn't give a shit about the story anyway. It only brought the lovebirds closer together.

IZZY. (*Rising.*) She still really wants kids as bad as she ever did, right?

ANNIE. (*Caught off guard.*) Uh—yeah. Yeah, I would say so.

IZZY. So what's the big secret?

ANNIE. Secret?

IZZY. Annie, you are a really bad liar. It's a sperm bank, right? No. Wait a minute. A genius sperm bank. Now that would be just like her. She'll pay extra for genius sperm.

ANNIE. Izzy, what on earth are you talking about now?

IZZY. Chuck can't have kids, can he? I know that's the big secret between you. I was right all along. Just admit it.

ANNIE. Izzy. I assure you. You are definitely not right. You are way off the mark about this. Trust me.

IZZY. Let's see. It goes something like this. She's marrying this dickless rich guy who'll pay all the bills, in exchange for an agreement. When the happy couple gives

birth to a bundle of joy, the world will think he's the
fertile Daddy-o, only the happy couple will know in secret
that the real Daddy is faceless and nameless, since they
bought the sperm for a hefty price. Monica, on the other
hand, revels in the idea that between them, she then is the
only true parent of the bundle of joy, which gives her total
control over the hopeless male-female power struggle that
we all had shoved down our throats every day of our lives.
Don't you get it, Annie? What better way to get back at
Dad than to rip his face off? She's doin' a Mom and Dad
hate step with this dickless guy, only without the punches
and kicks.

ANNIE. Izzy. Would you like to give me a clue as to
what you're saying.

*(Pause. IZZY pulls the diary out of her pocket, throws it
on the table. It is still wrapped in tape.)*

ANNIE. What is that?

IZZY. Monica's diary.

ANNIE. Oh my God! You didn't read her diary on top
of everything else, did you?

IZZY. Even I draw the line somewhere, Annie.

ANNIE. Where did you get it?

IZZY. Roger.

ANNIE. Roger?

IZZY. He's down the street. He showed up last night in
a total crazy sweat, talkin' about wringing Monica's neck.
I think he's gonna ask her to marry him.

ANNIE. What?! Where is he now?

IZZY. Beats me. Me and Joel took him to the Inn, he
was really strung out.

ANNIE. He said he'd be back?

IZZY. First thing.

ANNIE. Maybe he overslept.

IZZY. Want me to go get him?

ANNIE. No. Not yet. I mean—oh, my God, I don't know what I mean! Why didn't you wake me up?

IZZY. I am so depressed, Annie. How can she still wanna marry this dickless guy and—give up totally for herself on something beautiful that must exist in the universe someplace, doesn't it? I mean, if you and she can't make it with a guy then I never will. That means the crazy man fucked us all up permanently, didn't he?

ANNIE. No! He did not!

IZZY. Well then why would she choose a sperm bank over a person?

ANNIE. She hasn't and she won't. I'm positive. The machinery in question has already worked, at least once. (*ANNIE eyes her pointedly.*)

IZZY. What do you mean.

ANNIE. What do you think I mean.

IZZY. Don't make me guess, whaddaya mean?

ANNIE. You won't blab it to all the guests and anybody who passes by in the street?

IZZY. Annie!

ANNIE. I mean you really won't tell anyone else about it?

IZZY. Okay! What?

(*Pause.*)

ANNIE. Monica is pregnant.

IZZY. What?

ANNIE. Monica is pregnant. You know, carrying a baby.

IZZY. Her own baby?

ANNIE. (*Mocking.*) No! Someone else's!

IZZY. (*Dramatically upset.*) I am a hideous person! I am a hideous, hideous person! Is it really Chuck's? No question?

ANNIE. Uh-huh.

IZZY. I take back everything I said, if there's a baby involved, she's gotta marry him.

ANNIE. That's ridiculous!

IZZY. Wait a minute. That is ridiculous. How do you know it's Chuck's?

ANNIE. She told me.

IZZY. And you believe her?

ANNIE. Why shouldn't I?

(*Pause.*)

IZZY. Wait a minute. (*Remembering, grabbing the diary, tearing the tape off wildly.*) Oh, my God! Oh, Annie! Wow! Oh, wow, oh wow, oh wow! Fuck! She did lie! Wait until you hear this! Just wait!

ANNIE. You did read it! You just told me you didn't read it!

IZZY. (*Struggling with the tape.*) I lied.

ANNIE. Oh, that is just awful! Really, Izzy, that is just awful!

IZZY. (*Still tearing.*) Grow up, Annie! Any person in their right mind would read it. To tell you the truth, I question Roger's sanity for not reading it when Monica purposely left it behind for him to snoop! And then he tapes it shut like this? Is he a maniac or what? I can't get over it! (*SHE opens it, flips.*) Listen!

ANNIE. Oh, no! Not more!

IZZY. (*Reads, intense.*) Journal entry March fifteenth, three months ago. "Finally had sex with Roger last night, even though I hate him."

(*ANNIE makes an exasperated sound, IZZY waves it off, continues reading.*)

IZZY. "At the rate we're going, it will probably be the last time ever so I took my chances"—get that, Annie, she TOOK HER CHANCES— "and will see after all if Roger and I have any fate together." Can you believe this? Can you believe she did this?

ANNIE. Izzy, you're driving me crazy!

IZZY. It gets better! (*Reads.*) "Roger would kill me first and then die if he knew, so maybe there will never be a reason to tell him. Why should he ever know that what he can give me Chuck cannot." (*Lowering the book.*) Do you believe this, Annie? Do you believe she had the balls to do this?

ANNIE. Do what, I'm a wreck!

IZZY. "What Chuck cannot"! Sperm! She stole those fertile little devils right outta Roger!

ANNIE. Do you think Chuck knows?

IZZY. Of course he knows!

ANNIE. How can you be sure, what if it did work once and he is the father?

IZZY. No, Annie, no! "What Chuck cannot"! This is proof of what that ex-wife told Joel! Monica is lying!

Chuck's been married twice before and he has no children, right?

ANNIE. Right.

IZZY. (*Delighted.*) Because he can't have children, there's something wrong with his dick!

ANNIE. Izzy!

IZZY. Come on, Annie, Roger is the father and she's not even gonna tell him! She told the scumbag sleazeball only so she could make a business deal!

ANNIE. You can't be sure of that yet! You don't know for sure!

IZZY. (*Shoving the book at her.*) Look at it!

ANNIE. (Shoving it back.) I can't look at it, I'm gonna throw up!

IZZY. (*Takes it, takes tape.*) I'm gonna get Roger.

ANNIE. No! Stay out of it! She'll kill you!

IZZY. All right, then I'll go get Joel to confirm it!

ANNIE. Wait a minute! ... You mean that bitch lied to me and everybody except Chuck?!

IZZY. That's right.

ANNIE. Boy, does that suck!

IZZY. That's it, Annie! Get mad!

ANNIE. Okay. Okay if this is true I'm gonna be pissed but—maybe she has a reason. Maybe she's been planning to tell Roger herself.

IZZY. When? AFTER the ceremony?

ANNIE. Oh, how am I supposed to know?

IZZY. I know, Annie. Trust me on this one because I'd do the same thing. That's what really gets me! She planned on never telling Roger the truth because any baby of hers would just be a reject even before it was born, like her! ... I always felt like Dad hated me the most, but I guess she—she really does feel unlovable too.

(Pause.)

ANNIE. We still can't be the ones to tell him about that baby.

(HARRY appears on the porch behind them, nicely dressed. HE waits a moment, goes to the screen door.)

IZZY. *(Going to the door with diary and tape, excited.)* I'm getting Roger anyway!

ANNIE. Izzy, you can't!

IZZY. I won't tell him, I'm just gonna bring him— *(At the door, seeing him.)* Harry! Hiya, Harry.

HARRY. Can I come in?

IZZY. Annie?

ANNIE. *(Rising.)* Yeah. Uh—yeah, come in.

(HE enters, ANNIE smiles, awkward. Realizing her clothes:)

ANNIE. Excuse the appearance.

HARRY. At least you're appearing.

IZZY. I'll be back as soon as I can, he's just up the street!

ANNIE. Hurry!

(IZZY exits out the porch door.)

ANNIE. (*Goes to the sink with her dishes.*) Come in. Sit down. Something.

HARRY. You're not gonna run up the steps?

ANNIE. I'm gonna wait a few minutes before I do this time.

HARRY. Keep me guessing.

ANNIE. Not really.

HARRY. (*Pause. Comes nearer, watchful.*) Has Monica gotten a chance to try the strawberry galettes yet?

ANNIE. (*With a laugh.*) Come on, Harry.

HARRY. They might be funny to you, to me it's serious business if a client isn't happy. Has she tried them?

ANNIE. I'm sure they're fine.

HARRY. You mean she didn't rave about how good they were and fall over dead?

ANNIE. I'm sure she will when she gets a chance. (*Pause.*) You want some coffee, juice, alcohol?

HARRY. Coffee'd be nice.

ANNIE. O-kay. (*SHE gets cup, spoon, coffee, napkin during following.*) Same as before?

HARRY. Same as before. (*HE sits. Pause.*) So how are you, Annie? All I really wanted to know was how you were.

ANNIE. Good. Very happy alone, really. Very, very—well not THAT happy but happy.

HARRY. The work's going well?

ANNIE. Uh-huh.

HARRY. (*Delighted.*) I knew it, I always knew it would! I just happen to be following the art scene in Los Angeles, because, you know, I just opened one of my stores there, so I've seen your reviews, I've read about your—talking sculptures. I'd love to see them, they sound—well, they sound positively ridiculous and wonderful.

ANNIE. They are both.

HARRY. (*Teasing.*) Modest.

ANNIE. Modesty doesn't pay.

HARRY. Neither does a grudge.

ANNIE. It's not a grudge, Harry, it's a total lack of trust.

HARRY. How can you be proven wrong if you won't give me another chance?

(Pause. ANNIE shrugs.)

HARRY. Is there someone else?

ANNIE. I'm too old for someone else. Why keep trying at something you're lousy at.

HARRY. I guess not.

ANNIE. Right.

(Pause.)

HARRY. Annie, I'll say it again. I'll say it a million times if it'll help. If I had anything to do with you going to the hospital, I'm sorry. I was young and stupid and I'm sorry.

ANNIE. Repetition is not the answer.

HARRY. What is?

(Pause.)

ANNIE. I don't know how to forgive you. If I do I'm afraid the earth will suddenly open up and swallow me. I'll disappear.

HARRY. No, Annie. With or without me you'll never disappear again, I know just by looking at you.

ANNIE. Looks can be deceiving.

HARRY. Could you return one of my calls, answer one of my letters?

ANNIE. A more reasonable person would've taken silence as a message.

HARRY. Can you say you don't love me? Say it only if it's true and I'll go away. I'll leave you alone and—happy.

(Pause.)

ANNIE. *(Moving away.)* Look, Harry. I can't think about this. You don't understand what's going on here today. Monica is—well, Monica is ... Never mind!

HARRY. Monica's in trouble.

ANNIE. No!

HARRY. She's upset. Is it the food?

ANNIE. No!

HARRY. Just checking. Can I help?

ANNIE. Monica should probably not be doing what she's about to do.

HARRY. She should marry Roger.

ANNIE. No! I mean, yes, maybe, but that's not what I mean. How do you know?

HARRY. She probably loves him.

ANNIE. Oh, well, fine, love. Big deal, love! What a crock! That's not all it takes, you know. Fidelity to some is also desirable. I can't imagine why, of course, but it is.

(Pause.)

HARRY. I personally plan on being faithful to my wife. Go on.

ANNIE. Well so she's—she's doing the wrong thing. I mean if in fact it is the wrong thing.

HARRY. Is Chuck an alcoholic?

ANNIE. No!

HARRY. Is he violent?

ANNIE. Never!

HARRY. Is he unfaithful?

ANNIE. Of course not!

HARRY. (*Seizing his opportunity.*) You mean there's a worse crime under the sun than making one sad little slip of infidelity when your fiancée lied to you and told you that she herself had been unfaithful when in fact she hadn't, she just made you think she was to test you and you failed that test in a fit of panic? ... Of course she set you up to fail her, but you forgave her for that because you knew she was scared, she was terrified of marrying a man like her father and rightly so. Now, you regret in the deepest fibers of your being that cowardly slip you made and you know you'll never do it again if she would only forgive you, if she would only give you another chance. You mean to tell me there's something more unforgivable under the sun than having been terrified in your twenties of a lifelong commitment to a person who didn't believe it was possible?

(Pause.)

ANNIE. I suppose there is, yes.

HARRY. God, I want a witness!

ANNIE. You just want to win! You've always had to win, Harry. Admit it.

HARRY. I care more now about two things. Food and you. Not in that order. If you refuse to have me now I still plan on taking over the world with my food.

ANNIE. Not so fast, I'm not gonna just resume!

HARRY. You're gonna deliberate for the next five years?

ANNIE. Let me think! Let me think now and deal with this wedding! ... I do have to stop my sister from ruining her own chances, I do! *(Pause. ANNIE looks out screen door, upset.)* She's setting herself up to confirm that she's—unlovable, like he said.

HARRY. She's always listened to you. Tell her she's not.

ANNIE. *(Looking out.)* Here come Izzy and Joel!

HARRY. Would you get her to try the strawberry galettes?

ANNIE. You'd better go.

HARRY. Go? Do I have to wait five years to call you?

ANNIE. Tomorrow.

HARRY. Tomorrow?

ANNIE. Tomorrow, Harry. That's it, take it or leave it! *(SHE opens the door for him to leave. Pause. THEY grin at each other, laugh.)* You have something against tomorrow?

HARRY. No. (*HE grabs her face, kisses her passionately and quickly.*) It's about time. (*HARRY exits.*)

(*Barely a moment passes before IZZY enters from the porch with JOEL right behind her. ANNIE holds the door, closes it behind them. JOEL is not dressed for the wedding. IZZY has put the diary back in her pocket.*)

IZZY. (*To Annie, entering.*) I saw that! Whew! (*SHE hugs her impulsively.*)

ANNIE. Hi Joel.

JOEL. Hello Annie.

ANNIE. (*To Izzy.*) I thought you were getting Roger.

IZZY. Joel was on his way here to talk to me. Roger left already.

ANNIE. No! He left without seeing her?

IZZY. His bag's still there. Joel thinks he just went for a walk.

JOEL. He's a very unpredictable and strange person, if anybody wants my opinion.

IZZY. They don't.

ANNIE. I'll get dressed. (*SHE goes to the steps.*) I'll get dressed but there's not gonna be a wedding anyway.

IZZY. Monica's decided?!

ANNIE. No.

IZZY. Has she come down?

ANNIE. No.

IZZY. You went up?

ANNIE. No.

IZZY. Have you talked to her?

ANNIE. No! I just decided! (*ANNIE exits up the steps.*)

(JOEL and IZZY stare after her, gaping. Pause.)

JOEL. She still hasn't cancelled the wedding?

IZZY. Guess not.

JOEL. This shocks me. I've gotta tell you, Isabelle. This really shocks me. *(HE sits, disturbed. Pause.)*

IZZY. What do you need to tell me, Joel?

JOEL. Tell you?

IZZY. You just said—as you chased me up the street like a puppy dog—that you had something to tell me?

JOEL. Oh! I got my confirmation call this morning, so I just called my editor, and the story's definitely running on Sunday, with a double byline.

IZZY. *(Sitting, stricken.)* Shit!

JOEL. This is—really not the reaction most editorial assistants would have, believe me.

IZZY. Which name comes first.

JOEL. Yours.

IZZY. Really?

JOEL. Well, it's—alphabetical.

IZZY. "Isabelle Bowlin," just like that on the front page, spelled right and everything?

JOEL. Uh-huh.

IZZY. Wow! Thanks, Joel.

JOEL. You're welcome. I'm glad to see you finally smile about it. If I had known I was gonna be up half the night with you over it, I might've thought twice about talking my editor into—no, I woulda talked him into it anyway.

IZZY. So why did you go way out there on that limb for me?

JOEL. I told you, you deserve it, that's all, it's just right!

IZZY. You don't want a date with my sister in return?

JOEL. Excuse me?!

IZZY. So. If we're done with business, I don't wanna keep you here or anything. Guess I'll see you this week? Partner?

JOEL. (*Moving towards the steps.*) Yeah, uh—look, Isabelle. Now that it's definitely running tomorrow, do you think it would be inappropriate for me to have a word with Monica? It would just take a few minutes.

IZZY. What are you gonna say?

JOEL. Well, uh—just that I'm sorry, but—what's true is true, and I hope that there are no hard feelings.

IZZY. Then are you gonna ask her for a date?

JOEL. Isabelle! I really don't think that this would be the proper psychological moment to ask your sister for a date, do you?

IZZY. I don't know. Chuck's a scumbag, the wedding's a joke, and Roger's probably crazy. Maybe it's your moment.

JOEL. You know, I think he is crazy. I was listening to him last night—I mean, not really listening, I happened to hear him several times in the hallway last night because—you know, in these old houses the walls are thin, and—he was talking to himself. Loudly. Can you imagine having a dialogue with yourself in some strange hallway in the middle of the night?

IZZY. Probably.

JOEL. Oh, Isabelle. You have a much better grip on things than that.

IZZY. Glad somebody thinks so.

JOEL. Oh, come on! I mean—the two of these guys! Both of them! I mean—they are really—not much!

IZZY. People act strange when they're in love, Joel.

JOEL. I—don't know if that's what it is.

IZZY. That's what it is. You don't know shit about your heart, do you?

JOEL. Look. All I'm trying to get in is another apology, plain and simple.

IZZY. No, Joel.

JOEL. I'd just like to make sure she doesn't hold anything against me in case we—work together someday.

IZZY. (*Gently.*) You're not gonna get what you want, Joel. (*Pause.*) I can appreciate it because I'd rather live in my big fantasies too than have to wonder why I keep smackin' up against the sad little reality of nobody. I never want anybody who would want me either. I can't even get you to look at me and I've tried everything. It's okay. If you did I wouldn't know what to do with you anyway, I'd just fuck it up. I've decided I'm gonna learn how to take care of myself first. Somehow, I'm gonna learn how to take care of myself.

JOEL. (*Going to the door, mortified.*) I guess you'll— clear the air for me.

IZZY. I'll make sure she holds nothin' against you.

JOEL. Thanks, Isabelle.

IZZY. (*With amazement.*) Thank you, Joel. You're a real pal.

JOEL. Good luck.

IZZY. Good-bye.

(JOEL exits out the porch.)

IZZY. (*Looks after him a moment, thoughtful. To herself, happily:*) Who cares if he wants her and not me? What's it to me?

PAT. (*Looks in from porch.*) Izzy?! (*PAT enters with a calculator and legal pad and pencil.*) Izzy, she's got to see these figures. Under the circumstances, he is a very bad bet.

IZZY. She's not going through with it!

PAT. I should say not! She'd have to support him!

IZZY. We're stopping her. Annie and I are gonna stop her.

PAT. Well, thank God. According to my attorney's calculations, he stands to lose every single one of his millions in approximately two years, after a very long and complex trial in which he will have to testify against ten colleagues just to save his own hide.

IZZY. Do you think I should go up?

PAT. If you don't, I will.

MONICA. (*Before Izzy answers, MONICA rushes down the back steps and enters. SHE wears the buttoned wedding dress. Her face is flushed and more made up.*) Izzy, why is Annie refusing to talk to me?!

IZZY. You put up the wall first!

MONICA. I'm up there shaking like a leaf, I can't even get my eyeliner on straight because I don't have your— what are you telling Annie now?!

IZZY. What'd you forget to tell us, never mind Roger.

MONICA. (*Pause.*) I have no idea what you're talking about. All I know is that I need you and Annie to support my decision even if it turns out to be the wrong thing.

IZZY. Why?

PAT. (*Pause.*) Monica, you should really take a quick but careful glance at these figures. In two years Chuck is going to have the net worth of your average bag man.

MONICA. I don't care!

PAT. (*To Izzy.*) This is serious!

(*MONICA groans, gets some bubbly water from the fridge and sips it, pacing, calming herself.*)

IZZY. Do you wanna listen to me or do you wanna bark at me?

MONICA. Make it quick, this isn't even half the make-up!

IZZY. Could we talk alone Pat?

PAT. What's to say, just show her these! (*SHE waves the papers.*)

MONICA. Please, Pat!

PAT. (*Shoving the papers at Izzy as SHE goes.*) I'll be outside!

(*PAT exits. IZZY puts the papers down.*)

MONICA. Nothing you can say can change my mind.

IZZY. Why do you need my support if I'm so fuckin' unimportant?

MONICA. (*Demands.*) What!

(*Pause.*)

IZZY. I—understand I'm pretty naive about things. I guess part of growing up is realizing that you can't expect to get everything in a marriage.

MONICA. Well, bully for you!

IZZY. I'm gonna ignore your insults. I'm just gonna—plow ahead like a grown up.

MONICA. Point, please!

IZZY. I understand why you're trying to marry a man who appears to be a willing father, but that kid is gonna wind up feeling pretty much the same despair you do about connecting in a deep way with another human being!

MONICA. Oh, this is not relevant! Izzy, no one gets deep! Most people get tired and settle for shallow with a lot of safety and co-operation. You get lucky like me and get that, you fill in the rest of the picture with the image of happiness and forget it. It's close enough.

IZZY. I don't believe you.

ANNIE. (*Pause. ANNIE, wearing her maid of honor dress, enters. SHE has snuck down the back steps and was listening in the hall.*) Me neither.

MONICA. (*Cynically.*) Oh, great! This is just great! Two against one two hours before my wedding. I can't be anybody other than who I am!

ANNIE. (*To Izzy.*) Should we tell her we know?

IZZY. I think so!

MONICA. Know what?

ANNIE. Monica, do you know that Chuck can't be a biological father?

(*Pause. MONICA moves away abruptly.*)

ANNIE. Monica? Monica, you do know, don't you?

MONICA. (*Not looking at her.*) That's ridiculous.

ANNIE. Is it?

(Pause.)

MONICA. What difference does it make.

ANNIE. *(Very disappointed.)* Oh, God! Why would you do this?

MONICA. Arrest me! Go ahead, arrest me! All along he's wanted the baby just as much! More! He'll be a better father, you guys just refuse to believe me.

IZZY. So Chuck's known all along that it's Roger's?

MONICA. Of course!

IZZY. But he doesn't want the world to know, right? That's part of your deal, right?

MONICA. So what?!

IZZY. Don't you think that's more about his huge fuckin' ego than about wanting to nurture and love a human being, Monica?

MONICA. Ohh—No!

(IZZY exchanges a meaningful glance with ANNIE. Pause.)

ANNIE. And Roger really has no idea?

MONICA. If he doesn't want me, I'm not gonna blackmail him with a kid. Jesus, Annie! How low do you want me to sink!

ANNIE. I think Izzy's right about Chuck, Monica. A man who really wanted to love a child for the child's sake wouldn't really care what anyone thought.

MONICA. Oh, what difference does it make? Christ, what difference does it make?! *(Pause. MONICA plops into a chair, in despair.)* So Roger is right! I'm angry and selfish and determined to wreck everything! I couldn't tell him, I couldn't face him, he'd kill me! I took a chance because things were just so bad between us, they just fell apart and I was just so scared! I don't see Chuck that way. I mean, I'm not even sure he is that way. I just thought I'd never get another chance, you know, another chance?! Oh, I am just horrible, I am just so horrible!

ANNIE. Now, Monica, you are not.

MONICA. I am! I can't believe I did it! But the way I saw it, see, I mean, when I couldn't have the abortion and Chuck wanted me because I was pregnant and everything, was that maybe the kid would be very happy after all. I mean maybe it would be a mercenary type kid, and the trust fund would kinda—make up for the lack of love. Couldn't maybe the trust fund make up for the lack of love?

IZZY. Whose lack of love, Monica? The lack of love your baby might suffer from or the lack of love you're suffering from?

MONICA. Oh, haven't I gotten enough—things?! I have over two hundred pairs of shoes!

IZZY. That baby will just be another thing to Chuck, Monica. Another thing he can own.

ANNIE. And dominate.

MONICA. Oh, you guys can't know that!

ANNIE. Are you gonna cancel this wedding, Monica?

MONICA. No!

ANNIE. No?!

(ANNIE and IZZY exchange a worried glance.)

ANNIE. At the very least, doesn't Roger have a right to know?!

MONICA. He has no rights! (*Pause.*) Well, he has other rights as a human being but I can't just walk out on Chuck now. Life is a series of compromises!

ANNIE. In which you should never compromise yourself.

IZZY. Like Mom did.

MONICA. I'm not like Mom! I mean—there is no violence here! No violence.

(*Pause.*)

ANNIE. Couldn't Roger be kinda happy to learn about this?

MONICA. Are you kidding? He'd kill me, I tell you, he would fucking kill me!

(*Pause. IZZY and ANNIE exchange a worried glance. MONICA sees it.*)

MONICA. Wait a minute. What is this? How'd you guys know? How'd you even know it was his in the first place?!

ANNIE. Show her, Izzy.

IZZY. (*Pulls the diary out of her pocket, throws it on counter.*) You practically drew him a diagram.

MONICA. (*Grabbing it.*) What is—that's my diary! Where'd you get this? I was looking all over for this! Eew! There's sticky stuff all over it. Who the hell put tape all over it?

IZZY. Roger.

MONICA. Roger?

IZZY. You left it at his place, Monica. He didn't read it, he taped it up like a maniac. He's down the street, he got here last night and came here and gave it to me.

MONICA. He's down the street?! Why?!

IZZY. He wants to talk to you. I think he wants to ask you to marry him.

MONICA. What?!

IZZY. That's why he's here.

MONICA. Did he say that?

IZZY. No. He said he was in traffic.

MONICA. (*Flipping through the book, frantic.*) That can't be why he's here, he hates me! He screamed at me, right in front of the moving men, that he hated me and then he went into the bedroom and locked the door. (*SHE finds the page, reads.*) Oh, my God. (*SHE shuts it, puts the book in the closest drawer and slams it shut, frantic.*) He's here to kill me!

IZZY. Monica, get a grip.

ANNIE. Monica! Monica, he didn't even read it!

MONICA. (*Closing and locking the door.*) Somebody make sure the front door's locked!

IZZY. Monica, I swear he didn't read it! He said he wasn't gonna play any more games, he's had it with that shit! There were so many feet of masking tape on the goddamn book it took me half an hour to get it off!

MONICA. (*Races around room, checks the windows.*) I guess I'll have to hide!

ANNIE. Monica!

MONICA. (*Reaches the steps.*) Don't let him in! When he shows up, do not let him in.

ANNIE. Monica! STOP RIGHT THERE!

(MONICA stops. At the same time, ROGER appears on the porch, unseen. HE collects himself a minute, scared.)

ANNIE. Has he ever hit you?
MONICA. Not yet.
ANNIE. Then why are you acting like he has? Just because a person is hurt and has a temper, that doesn't mean that they'd ever—

(ROGER comes to the door. ANNIE sees him.)

ANNIE. Roger!
ROGER. Annie. Is uh—is Monica here?

(IZZY should be close enough to MONICA to grab her wrist, keep her from going up the steps.)

ANNIE. Yes! Yes. She's—she's right here, Roger. She's—over there.
MONICA. (*Terrified.*) Annie please!

(ANNIE opens the screen door. ROGER enters. HE is terrified, awkward. Pause. As soon as MONICA sees him SHE stops fighting IZZY, acts like nothing happened, fixes her appearance.)

ROGER. Hi Monica.
MONICA. Hi.
IZZY. (*Pause. IZZY goes to the screen door by Annie.*) Roger.
ROGER. Isabelle.

MONICA. Where you going.

IZZY. Right outside here. We'll be right outside here, just a few feet away, don't worry.

ANNIE. (*To Monica.*) With clubs, just in case.

(ANNIE and IZZY exit to the porch, as far as they can go but not very far and sit, within sight, facing out. IZZY smokes cigarettes. ROGER notes them, confused. MONICA fixes her dress, puts things in sink.)

ROGER. Is there someplace—a little more private where we could talk?

MONICA. No.

ROGER. Good start, Monica. Good start.

MONICA. Make it fast, Roger. I have a ceremony to attend.

ROGER. (*Pause. ROGER comes further into the room, leans on a counter, exhausted.*) I'm sorry I overslept, I got here last night.

MONICA. You weren't invited.

ROGER. You seem a little rattled.

MONICA. (*Hardly looking at him.*) You look like shit.

ROGER. Thanks.

MONICA. Anytime.

ROGER.(*Pause.*) Monica, I think we should just stop all the bullshit and just plunge in and get married.

MONICA. What?

ROGER. Married. You and me.

MONICA. (*With a laugh.*) Roger, I'm already getting married. That's what this ceremony is today, it's a wedding ceremony. There's a tent the size of Texas in the backyard. I'm wearing a wedding dress. Note the white?

ROGER. Please don't talk to me like that. Please, Monica, gimme a fuckin' break.

MONICA. Well, I'm just a little amazed. I mean, talk about waiting until the last minute.

ROGER. When you get that tone with me, you know I start shouting even though I don't want to. I told myself today that no matter what happened, no matter what you said to me, I would not shout.

MONICA. Well, aren't I the lucky one today! I'm not gonna be treated like a dog.

ROGER. Neither one of us would abuse a dog the way we abuse each other, Monica, and it's gonna stop. It's gonna stop right now.

MONICA. (*Pause. MONICA crosses to the table, sits.*) I can't believe you came.

ROGER. Neither can I.

MONICA. You drove the whole way?

ROGER. Yup.

MONICA. Where'd you stay.

ROGER. Some—Inn up the street. Heard you got bad news last night. This guy's a crook?

MONICA. (*With a shrug.*) Guess so.

ROGER. Why would you wanna marry a crook.

MONICA. I don't know. Makes me feel protected.

ROGER. (*Pause.*) You're such a blockhead. I'm sorry I didn't come to your birthday party. I'm sorry I lose my temper and call you a bitch and I'm sorry I shouted at you in front of the moving men.

MONICA. I'm sorry for everything. I am a bitch.

ROGER. Oh, you're not that bad.

MONICA. I'm sorry I abandoned you. I guess I should've warned you first.

ROGER. (*Dissolving, coming over to embrace her with open arms.*) Oh, Monica! Ho-ney! We can make it, can't we? Now we're getting somewhere. Aren't we getting somewhere here?

MONICA. (*Jumping up, pulling away from him.*) No, Roger, no! I mean, we always get somewhere and then everything just busts apart, it just goes flyin' all around! You're too late. Do you understand? You're just too late.

ROGER. (*Pause. ROGER takes a moment, and then decisively pulls something out of his pocket. It is a ring, a gold wedding band. HE wipes it off, tries to give it to her.*) Here.

MONICA. (*Not taking it.*) What is that.

ROGER. A ring.

MONICA. (*With a laugh.*) I already have a ring. Sorry, Roger, but I have a real ring. See? (*SHE shows him the ring.*)

ROGER. (*HE puts his on the table.*) This one's better.

MONICA. God, Roger, you are unbelievable! We sat there for hours—humiliating ourselves in front of that doctor, you talking endlessly about how we should just get engaged, not get married for another year, not have kids until we were about a hundred, and now you expect me to just jump at this pathetic little carrot on the same day that I am supposed to marry someone else, someone who is really there for me?!

ROGER. You don't give two shits about this guy, and he is certainly not there for you.

MONICA. He is so! You don't know anything about it.

ROGER. After all we've been through together, the fact that you can look me in the eye and lie about some—prop of a guy makes me just wanna—

MONICA. Smack me?

ROGER. Throw up!

MONICA. Oh! What a delightful image.

ROGER. I'm breaking this fucked up pattern, Monica! I'm not playin' any games anymore, I'm gonna jump right in and marry you today if you want! Right now, right here, we can get married in that fuckin' tent, you and me, like we should have a long time ago.

MONICA. Oh, you are ridiculous!

ROGER. (*Shouts.*) STOP IT, MONICA! STOP FUCKING ABUSING ME SO I CAN ABUSE YOU BACK!

(*Pause. MONICA runs to the door, frightened. IZZY and ANNIE react outside, on alert, but don't come in.*)

MONICA. Please don't shout at me, Roger. Please don't shout.

ROGER. I'm not gonna shout! No matter what you say to me, I'm not gonna shout!

MONICA. God, I am totally lost.

ROGER. Then stop fighting it, Monica! Stop believing I'm gonna turn into your father because I raise my voice! I'm just like you, I have problems, I'm wounded, I'm scared to death, but I can get over it, I'm gonna get over it! If we keep at it, we can still get over it together, can't we? (*Pause.*) Will you marry me, Monica? Please? Pretty please? (*MONICA moves away, circles the table so that it is between them. Pause.*)

MONICA. No.

ROGER. No? Why not?

MONICA. You're not asking me in a very romantic way.

ROGER. Oh, for Christ's sake! What do you want from me? You moved out on me! It took everything I had to come here! I'm trying as hard as I can, please, what do you want from me?

MONICA. Unconditional, unequivocal, total acceptance and love. Something you will never be able to give to me.

ROGER. Oh, Monica! I'm not your fuckin' Daddy!

MONICA. Well I certainly didn't get that from him.

ROGER. I mean I cannot be the parent you never had, I'm just a person with a past, I'm not a saint!

MONICA. Maybe the wrong past, maybe both our pasts together are just totally impossible to manage.

ROGER. You want a concept, not a person!

MONICA. Maybe.

ROGER. Yes! You know that—thing, that step Doctor Mellman kept talking about? Like that we were like two five-year-olds on a diving board going, "you go first," "no, you go first," "no, you go first", so no one went first so no one ever got to experience how exhilarating it might be to just dive into the water and come up floating and supported?

MONICA. I hated that woman's imagery. All I kept thinking was, yeah, fine, but what if somebody forgot to fill the pool?

ROGER. There is water in the pool, Monica. She was right about this. Besides, I'm telling you, I'm diving in first, so I'll break my head if there's no water in the pool, but I'm not worried, because there's water in the pool!

MONICA. (*Pause.*) What about kids. Do we still have to be a hundred? I'm thirty-three, Roger. I'm already thirty-three years old.

ROGER. We should still wait on that one.

MONICA. Wait? How long?

ROGER. Couple of years.

MONICA. But I can't wait a couple of years, that's impossible, that's just impossible. (*Pause.*) I'm sorry, Roger, the answer just has to be no. Now I have a ceremony to attend if you'll excuse me. Thank you for— well, thank you for coming. (*SHE goes to the steps.*)

(*IZZY, hearing this exchange, comes close to the screen door. ANNIE tries to stop her but IZZY pulls away. IZZY waits at the door, unseen.*)

ROGER. "Thank you for coming?!" What the hell, did you just turn into a stewardess or something?

MONICA. Roger, I cannot wait to have children. Do you understand, I can not wait!

ROGER. (*Pause.*) Are you telling me you're pregnant?

MONICA. Yes.

ROGER. With his kid.

MONICA. (*Not looking at him.*) Yes.

ROGER. You're positive it's his.

MONICA. Yes.

ROGER. (*Pause.*) How long.

MONICA. Couple months.

ROGER. Couple months? Like eight weeks?

MONICA. More.

ROGER. How much more.

MONICA. Enough!

ROGER. Jesus, Monica. Was it an accident?

MONICA. Yes.

ROGER. Is it really too late to stop it?

MONICA. (*Shouts.*) I cannot and will not have an abortion!

(Pause.)

ROGER. Well I don't know what the hell to say. I don't know why the hell you took that chance except to just get back at me.

MONICA. Good-bye, Roger.

ROGER. You still don't have to marry the guy.

(IZZY enters through the screen door, forcefully. ANNIE is close behind her, enters and hangs by the door.)

IZZY. Monica, just tell him the truth.

MONICA. Izzy, I'll kill you!

ANNIE. Izzy, don't! Just don't.

ROGER. (*Pause.*) Monica. Monica, is it my kid?

IZZY. No.

MONICA. (*Simultaneous, without looking at him.*) No!

ANNIE. (*With a shrug.*) Guess not.

ROGER. Monica, please don't lie to me about this.

MONICA. (*To Roger.*) I'm not! You better go now.

IZZY. Wait outside, Roger. Just—wait outside in the back a minute, would ya?

MONICA. Stay the hell out of it, Izzy.

ROGER. (*To Monica.*) If you're lying about this, I swear, I'll—I'll—

MONICA. You'll what, Roger. You'll what.

ROGER. I don't know, I think I'll—I'll cry!

IZZY. (*Grabbing his arm.*) Get outta here, wait in the yard, okay?

ROGER. (*As HE goes.*) I'm not leaving, Monica. I'm not leaving yet!

IZZY. It'll be just a second.

ROGER. (*Shouts.*) I am not leaving!

MONICA. (*Shouts after him.*) You're insane!

(*ROGER exits out into the yard.*)

IZZY. (Waves him on.) Further! Go further!

(*HE hesitates, goes further towards the tent so that HE disappears.*)

IZZY. (*Calls:*) Thank you!

MONICA. Izzy, you are a lunatic!

IZZY. Yeah, well I'd rather be a lunatic than you, dimwit! You're like a seven-year-old trapped in a grown-up's body!

MONICA. At least I'm not a case of total inner and outer retarded development! You are out of control, undisciplined, pushy, destructive, crazy and a total mess! No wonder you can't get anywhere, you are your father's daughter!

IZZY. (*Pause.*) When things get scary, take a shit on the family dumpster.

MONICA. Leave me alone.

IZZY. I don't even think I like you, but lemme tell you you are definitely doing the wrong thing.

ANNIE. Izzy's trying to help you, Monica! What does it take to get through to you?

MONICA. Just get him outta here, Annie. There's nothing more to say. It's getting late, I'm not even ready.

ANNIE. He just asked you to marry him.

MONICA. So?

ANNIE. So isn't that what you want?

MONICA. (*Keeping her voice down.*) I can't tell him the truth, Annie. He'll go crazy if I tell him the truth.

ANNIE. I don't get that impression. I don't get that impression at all. (*To Izzy.*) Do you?

(*IZZY shakes her head vaguely, as if brushing it off.*)

ANNIE. Monica, I think you've got things all muddled up here. I don't think you're seeing things as they are.

MONICA. You don't even know him! You don't even know who he is! I mean, who he is inside.

IZZY. I do.

MONICA. Shut up.

IZZY. No, I mean, I do! I mean I agree with you, Monica. There's good reason to believe he's an animal. I know. I know because of something he said last night.

ANNIE. What do you mean.

MONICA. What'd he say.

IZZY. You don't wanna know. It's cruel.

MONICA. What.

IZZY. Same word and everything. Same word Dad used to say.

ANNIE. Oh my God.

MONICA. What?

IZZY. (*Pause.*) I can't tell you.

MONICA. Izzy! You little witch!

IZZY. Well now I'm definitely not gonna tell you.

MONICA. Izzy! If he said something important I think I oughtta know it, don't you?

(Pause.)

IZZY. I asked him why he didn't seem to wanna be the father of your children. I mean in a hurry.

ANNIE. Izzy, how could you?

IZZY. It's a fair question. Since it seems to be an issue.

MONICA. What'd he say.

(Pause.)

IZZY. Well, uh—he said because—well, because any child of yours would be—unlovable. Like you.

MONICA. (*With a shocked laugh.*) He did not say that. He did not say that at all.

(IZZY shrugs, moves away. ANNIE watches IZZY carefully, gets what she is doing.)

MONICA. That is a Dad word, that is not a Roger word. (*Pause.*) Did he really say that? Izzy, I have to know if Roger really said that.

IZZY. He's outside, ask him.

(IZZY exchanges a quick look with ANNIE, who looks away, knows it's a ploy.)

MONICA. Did he or did he not use such a word? (*Going to the door, frantic.*) If he used that word I'm gonna be furious! If he didn't use that word I'm gonna kill you! (*Calls.*) ROGER! ROGER. COME HERE! ROGER!

(*ROGER re-appears, comes to the steps of the porch. Over her shoulder:*)

MONICA. He didn't use that word, he couldn't have, I know him, he didn't! Goddamn it, if he did there's no point in going on with life! I have no judgement whatsoever!

(*MONICA marches out onto the steps, stops at the top, scared. IZZY and ANNIE rush to the door.*)

MONICA. Roger?! Roger, I have to know if you—how could you—did you use the word ... unlovable?
ROGER. (*Totally lost.*) In reference to what.
MONICA. Me, you asshole! Me!
ROGER. No! God, Monica! How could I use that word?! I wouldn't! Don't you know that? Don't you know that by now?

(*MONICA spins around, marches back into the kitchen, upset. SHE slams the door. ROGER comes up the steps.*)

ROGER. Monica?
MONICA. (*To Izzy.*) You fucking liar!
IZZY. This time I had a purpose.
MONICA. (*Locks the screen door from the inside. More to herself.*) It doesn't matter what he said or didn't say, does

it? It doesn't matter what anybody says to me, I always hear the same thing.

(ANNIE comforts Monica.)

ROGER. *(Tries the door.)* Monica, would you open the door?
ANNIE. Just a minute, Roger.

(ROGER waits.)

MONICA. *(Shaking her head.)* God, I'm an idiot! I'm a complete and total idiot!

(IZZY crosses room, leans against counter.)

MONICA. How can I get past this? I have to get past this in life! *(Shaking her head, very serious.)* This marriage is a bad move.
ANNIE. *(With a laugh.)* Yeah. Bad move.

MONICA. *(Starts to laugh with her. Laughing more as SHE goes.)* BAD move?! Try—try fucking rotten move, huh? It's a—bomb of a move, I mean really, what the hell am I thinking, getting married to some—cold egomaniac because I can't tell the living from the dead!

(THEY laugh. IZZY tries to resist but can't. Pause.)

ROGER. *(From outside.)* Monica, will you open the door please?
ANNIE. *(To Monica.)* I think you're gonna have to—

MONICA. Face to face.

(MONICA goes to the door. ROGER steps back. SHE goes out. IZZY and ANNIE rush to the door again, but try to look casual. Pause.)

MONICA. Roger. Roger this kid is—this kid is—
ROGER. Mine.
MONICA. Yes.
ROGER. Oh my God. (*Goes to the steps, collapses with his head in his hands.*) God, Monica, what am I gonna do with you?

(MONICA bursts out laughing with IZZY and ANNIE.)

MONICA. But I'm not unlovable and he didn't smack me!
ANNIE. Of course not!
IZZY. Hit him back anyway!

(THEY laugh.)

ROGER. (*Shakes his head, laughs.*) God!
MONICA. Can you believe it, Roger? Can you believe that I did this and I'm still not unlovable?!

(SHE pounds him on the back playfully. HE grabs her hand and SHE kind of falls into him, in an embrace. IZZY and ANNIE look away, trying to give them a private moment. It is very hard for Izzy.)

MONICA. I'm sorry.

ROGER. God, you're hard. Lovable but very hard.

(Pause.)

MONICA. *(Playful.)* So, uh—you wanna get married now?

(HE rises, stands in the yard looking at her, steps away.)

MONICA. Where you going?
ROGER. I don't wanna get married in that tent. I don't like orchids.
MONICA. Neither do I.

(Pause. ROGER wanders off.)

MONICA. Where you going?
ROGER. Just to think. I'll be out here, just out here, okay?
MONICA. Okay.

(HE exits into the yard. Pause. MONICA watches him. IZZY and ANNIE come onto the porch, slowly.)

IZZY. He wouldn't just leave, would he?
MONICA. Not right away.
ANNIE. Come on, Monica! You have a pretty good shot since you already survived this, don't you?
MONICA. Yeah. I guess so.

(Pause. IZZY moves away from them, in her own world. MONICA watches her.)

IZZY. Mom woulda freaked out if she'd been around to see this mess here today. Wouldn't she have just freaked out?

ANNIE. She'd laugh!

IZZY. She would?

MONICA. (*With a laugh.*) Oh, yes.

IZZY. I wish I could see her laugh.

(Pause. MONICA moves close to Izzy, tries to touch her. IZZY resists.)

MONICA. Izzy, I—well, if I were you, I don't know if I could ever forgive me for the way I treat you. I'm the one who's acted like my father's daughter, and you just helped me in return. Thank you.

IZZY. (*Moving away, afraid of crying.*) Shut up. Would you just shut up?

MONICA.(*Follows her, afraid but determined.*) Izzy?

IZZY. (*Turning to her, her resistance down.*) Isn't that what a family's supposed to do?

MONICA. I didn't know I had one. (*MONICA hugs Izzy. Pause.*) I better go cancel the ceremony. (*MONICA goes down the steps, determined.*) Are you guys hungry?

IZZY. Starving!

MONICA. I'll grab some chicken and those strawberry things!

(ANNIE gives Monica a pointed look and gestures playfully towards the street.)

MONICA. After.

ANNIE. Hurry!

IZZY. Run!

MONICA. *(With relief.)* Okay. Here I go. *(SHE runs off, exits.)*

Blackout

END OF PLAY

COSTUME PLOT
(Costume plot by Mimi Maxmen)

ISABELLE
Act I, sc. 1
teal green shorts
faded brown man's pocket-T shirt
wedding gown—worn unbuttoned
socks
red high tops
watch
small ring
stud earrings
assorted chains, necklaces
sc. 2
black/yellow/turquoise sequined halter dress
hose
yellow sequin 3 1/2" heels
earrings
watch
ring
large bead choker necklace
bracelet
Act II
aqua Maid of Honor dress
matching shoes
large aqua and straw picture hat
hose
pearls
pearl earrings
gloves

ANNIE BOWLIN
Act I, sc. 1
coral printed jumper

yellow short-sleeve T shirt
flats
watch
earrings
sc. 2
peach/magenta/pink silk chiffon skirt w/ matching top
hose
hand painted shoes
earrings
long necklace
ring
bracelet
LATER and Act II
white terry cloth robe
white summer weight men's pajamas (short bottoms)
bra
underwear
slippers
small stud earrings
seriously rumpled hair for Act II
LATER in Act II
blush-colored Maid of Honor dress
matching shoes
hose
blush and straw picture hat
gold chain w/ pearl drop necklace
earrings
gloves

MONICA BOWLIN
Act I, sc. 1
cream wool crepe Anne Klein suit
cream silk charmeuse blouse
hose
black patent and ivory Chanel shoes

Fendi purse
watch
necklaces
lapel pin
bracelet
The Ring
earrings
sunglasses
sc. 2
pale blush-pink long "Fortuny" dress
satin and sequin 3" heels
choker
center front pin
earrings
bracelet
ANNIE brings her some sort of jacket
Act II
wedding dress
wedding veil
gloves
hose
shoes
ADD pearls for 2nd entrance
pearl and rhinestone earrings

PAT WEINHARDT
Act I, sc. 1
black and white silk outfit w/ black knit top w/ matching
    multi-colored trim
hose
white w/ multi-color heels
white quilted Chanel purse
large necklace
large earrings
major rings

trendy watch
a couple of bracelets
pin
sunglasses
Act II
bright orange romper
black leggings w/ multi-color floral design
watch
a few gold chain bracelets
chain (necklace) w/ some sort of stone
rings
earrings
sandals

HARRY HOBSON
Act I, sc. 1
pale yellow cotton pullover
orange/white stripe short-sleeve seersucker shirt
blue pin-wale shorts
belt
top-siders
watch
Act II
blue-grey jacket
grey slacks
cream shirt
tie
dark socks
dark dress shoes
belt
watch

JOEL SILVERMAN
Act I, sc. 2
black jeans

maroon Hawaiian shirt
jacket (probably not worn)
socks
boots
watch
Act II
pink button-down oxford cloth shirt
tie
wear jacket

ROGER DOWLING
Act I
khaki slacks
faded blue T shirt
zip-front sweatshirt
socks
sneakers
watch
Act II
white T shirt

PROPERTY PLOT

Kleenex/small cloth/handkerchief
large box w/bouquet of roses,white orchids, baby's breath
bottles of mineral water/bubbly water
shopping bags filled w/packages
glasses: water, juice, drink
gin bottle
tonic water
ice cubes
other liquor bottles—liquor cabinet
vodka bottle
peaches (eaten nightly by Annie)
photographs
briefcase
cigarettes
overnight bag
bag w/taped up diary
empty bottle of vodka
tea kettle
cups
spoons
tea
pencils
legal pads
pen
nail file
coffee
mugs/cups
percolator
milk
sugar bowl
phone
juice, orange
Tylenol/aspirin bottle

napkins
box w/wedding ring
ashtrays
dish towel
sponges
dish soap
drying rack
mat for under drying rack of dishes
plates
silverware
ceramic pots
bottle water
toaster oven
purse for Izzy
purse for Monica
keys
compact
lipstick
hair brush
giant make-up kit containing mirror
calculator w/paper coming out
fan
trashcan
2 bags of groceries
1 bag of liquor
bread/toast
milk
muffins for Annie
lighter
tissues

Other Publications for Your Interest

A WEEKEND NEAR MADISON
(LITTLE THEATRE—COMIC DRAMA)
By KATHLEEN TOLAN

2 men, 3 women—Interior

This recent hit from the famed Actors Theatre of Louisville, a terrific ensemble play about male-female relationships in the 80's, was praised by *Newsweek* as "warm, vital, glowing . . . full of wise ironies and unsentimental hopes". The story concerns a weekend reunion of old college friends now in their early thirties. The occasion is the visit of Vanessa, the queen bee of the group, who is now the leader of a lesbian/feminist rock band. Vanessa arrives at the home of an old friend who is now a psychiatrist hand in hand with her naif-like lover, who also plays in the band. Also on hand are the psychiatrist's wife, a novelist suffering from writer's block; and his brother, who was once Vanessa's lover and who still loves her. In the course of the weekend, Vanessa reveals that she and her lover desperately want to have a child—and she tries to persuade her former male lover to father it, not understanding that he might have some feelings about the whole thing. *Time Magazine* heard "the unmistakable cry of an infant hit . . . Playwright Tolan's work radiates promise and achievement." (#25051)

PASTORALE
(LITTLE THEATRE—COMEDY)
By DEBORAH EISENBERG

3 men, 4 women—Interior
(plus 1 or 2 bit parts and 3 optional extras)

"Deborah Eisenberg is one of the freshest and funniest voices in some seasons."—Newsweek. Somewhere out in the country Melanie has rented a house and in the living room she, her friend Rachel who came for a weekend but forgets to leave, and their school friend Steve (all in their mid-20s) spend nearly a year meandering through a mental landscape including such concerns as phobias, friendship, work, sex, slovenliness and epistemology. Other people happen by: Steve's young girlfriend Celia, the virtuous and annoying Edie, a man who Melanie has picked up in a bar, and a couple who appear during an intense conversation and observe the sofa is on fire. The lives of the three friends inevitably proceed and eventually draw them, the better prepared perhaps by their months on the sofa, in separate directions. "The most original, funniest new comic voice to be heard in New York theater since Beth Henley's 'Crimes of the Heart.'"—N.Y. Times. "A very funny, stylish comedy."—The New Yorker. "Wacky charm and wayward wit."—New York Magazine. "Delightful."—N.Y. Post. "Uproarious . . . the play is a world unto itself, and it spins."—N.Y. Sunday Times. (#18016)